The Old Money Blueprint

Rewrite the Script. Build a Dynasty.

Samuel Turney

Century Tree Press

Published by **Century Tree Press**
www.centurytreepress.com

Cover art by Khushnood @ Klassic Designs

ISBNs

Paperback ISBN: 978-1-7645113-1-5
Hardcover ISBN: 978-1-7645113-0-8
eBook ISBN: 978-1-7645113-2-2

Fiction Notice

This book contains fiction. The names, characters, and incidents portrayed in it are the work of the author's imagination. Any resemblance to actual persons, living or dead, events, or localities is entirely coincidental.

Disclaimer of Liability and Warranty

No Financial or Legal Advice

The information contained in *The Old Money Blueprint* (the "Work") is for educational, entertainment, and informational purposes only. It is not intended to be, and does not constitute, financial, legal, tax, or investment advice.

The author, Samuel Turney, and the publisher, Century Tree Press, are not acting as your personal financial advisors, accountants, or attorneys. The strategies, structures, and philosophies discussed in this Work are based on the author's personal opinions and experiences. They may not be suitable for your specific situation.

Seek Professional Counsel

THE OLD MONEY BLUEPRINT

Financial and legal structures (including trusts, taxation, and property law) are highly complex and subject to change. You should distinctly understand that the author is not providing professional advice or services to you. Before making any financial or legal decisions, you should consult with a qualified professional who understands your specific jurisdiction, risk tolerance, and financial needs.

No Guarantees

References to specific financial outcomes, "Old Money" results, or wealth accumulation are for illustrative purposes only. Past performance of any strategy is not indicative of future results. The author and publisher make no warranties, expressed or implied, regarding the accuracy, completeness, or currency of the information provided.

Limitation of Liability

By reading this Work, you agree that the author and publisher shall not be held liable for any direct, indirect, punitive, special, incidental, or consequential damages arising directly or indirectly from any use of this material, which is provided "as is" and without warranties.

First Edition

Contents

Introduction

Something doesn't feel right.

I walk in the grocery store and see a "special" price on a bag of chips that's more than the regular price was two years ago. On the radio they are saying the economy is better than ever.

I hear mates or colleagues bragging because their house value went up by a hundred grand this year. The next minute they talk about how hard it is for their kid to find a place to live.

They celebrate the wall getting higher, not realizing their kids are on the other side of it.

I tell an old guy in the office where I bought my first home. It's in a shit-hole area because it's what I could afford.

He smiles and says "Good on you! My son just bought out there too. Getting a foot on the ladder is what counts!"

I smile back, but inside I'm thinking, *Wait a minute, you have two paid-off investment properties. You're sitting on millions in equity. Why are you letting your son sign a 30 year life sentence to live in a shit-hole?*

Something doesn't feel right. You've probably noticed it, too. It's a gnawing, undefinable sense that the advice we are being given is broken. That "normal" is not really normal.

You look at the math, and you think: *I'm doing everything right. So why does it feel like I can't get ahead?*

Something's missing from the equation.

That sense of unease? You aren't crazy. You're not imagining it. And you haven't failed.

The truth? The game has changed. You're just playing by rules that expired twenty years ago.

The View from the Bench

I'm not writing this from a cabana in Miami. I'm not a guru floating on a cloud of passive income, lecturing you about mindset and grinding while my assistant polishes my Lambo.

I'm writing this on my lunch break.

I'm sitting on a park bench wearing office clothes that need ironing. Next to me is an empty tin of tuna because I'm on a diet and I'm too cheap to buy lunch. Most of this book wasn't written in a study. It was written at the kitchen table, in the few hours of quiet I get each night after the kids are asleep.

My name is Sam. I'm 32 years old. I have two kids, a mortgage, an office job, and no university degree. By all standard metrics,

I'm a success story. I earn an upper middle-class salary. I live in Perth, a city that's been affordable and stable for decades.

I followed the rules. I got the job. I bought the house. And I was lucky in one specific way: I wasn't forced into "the script."

My parents are good people. They didn't pressure me to go to university or chase a safe corporate ladder. They didn't indoctrinate me with the idea that a degree equals success. But they also didn't catch the wind. They missed the "Golden Tailwind" that lifted so many in their generation. They bought high and sold low.

So I grew up watching the "standard advice" fail good people. I grew up skeptical. I wanted to do things my own way.

But even doing it my way, I realized recently that I was *terrified*.

I looked at the economy. I looked at the skyrocketing asset prices. And the truth hit me. Western society is rapidly dividing into two permanent castes: the *renter class* and the *landlord class*.

We are standing on a precipice. You and me. We might be the last generation that has the chance to secure a foothold for our family. If we miss this window, if we keep following the old, broken map, our kids will be locked out forever.

This fear is the seed of this book.

Old Money Redefined

When you hear "Old Money," you probably think of monocles, trust funds, and soft-handed people who never worked a day in their life.

That's not what this book is about.

This book isn't a budgeting guide. It isn't about skipping lattes or clipping coupons.

It's a complete assault on the modern way of life.

In this book, "Old Money" is a philosophy of resilience. It's the rejection of a culture that wants to turn our children into fragile, obedient consumers. It's about realizing that in a world that's falling apart, the only thing that will save us is the strength of our family line.

It's about loyalty. It's about shifting our focus from "How do I get rich?" to "How do we survive?" It's about building a family culture so strong that it acts as a fortress against the chaos of the outside world.

Yes, I will talk about money. I will talk about the mathematical blueprint to build serious, dynastic wealth. But money is just the ammunition.

The mission is freedom.

The Roadmap

This book isn't a collection of random tips. It's a journey designed to take you from the *scripted* world to the *builder* world. From team *consumer* to team *producer.*

Part I: The Wake-Up Call - I'll show you the math you weren't supposed to see. I'll expose the blind spot—the financial trap that's designed to harvest your family's wealth without you even questioning it.

Part II: The Great Unlearning - I will tear down the cultural lies you were fed about debt, hobbies, education, and marriage. And I will replace the old map with a new philosophy.

Part III: The Builder's Blueprint - This is the "How." I will give you the practical, step-by-step system (The Builder's Waterfall) to manage your money, destroy your debt, and plant your Century Tree.

My Goal for This Book

You might be wondering: *If you've found a way to build a fortress for your family, why are you telling me? Why not just keep your head down and get rich quietly?*

The answer is not money.

The truth is, I am writing this for my grandchildren.

I don't want them to be the only ones who are free.

I want them to grow up in a world where they can find friends, partners, and spouses who share their values. I want them to live in a world where intergenerational wealth is a choice, not a fantasy.

If I'm the only one who builds this, my family is an island. But if you build this too—and your neighbor, and your brother, and your friend—then we are an archipelago. We are a culture.

I'm writing this to recruit you to that culture.

A Warning Before We Begin

As you read this book, you are going to feel resistance.

Maybe when I talk about your job, or the "investment" you made in your car, or when I say you should influence who your children marry. You will feel a spike of anger.

You'll want to close the book. You'll want to dismiss me as extreme, unrealistic, or a heretic.

This is not *you* thinking. This is the script defending itself.

The script acts like an immune system. It attacks any idea that threatens its survival.

The feeling of disgust is just the antibody.

Look, I'm not asking you to agree with everything I say. I'm not your guru. I don't want followers. I want fellow heretics.

A heretic questions everything, including me.

So when you feel your anger spike, don't close the book. *Lean in*. Ask yourself: "Why is the script trying so hard to protect this specific belief?"

That is where the real work begins.

Grab a shovel. We have a legacy to build.

Disclaimer

I am a Risk and Compliance professional by trade, which means I know exactly where the line is. Let me be clear: I am not your advisor. I am a father sharing his notes. The strategies in this book are powerful tools, but like any tool, they can cause damage if mishandled. Use them responsibly, and always get a second opinion from a qualified professional who works for you.

Part I: The Wake-Up Call

Century Tree Press

Chapter 1
THE FEVER DREAM

The First Link

A warm afternoon breeze moves across the porch, carrying the optimistic smell of spring growth and the distant, smoky hint of a family barbecue.

On the porch of the modest home stand two men, father and son.

The father, a man in his mid-fifties, holds out a small set of house keys. He is in casual clothes, but his hands tell the story of his life. They are large and strong, the palms and knuckles calloused and scarred- not from violence, but from decades of work. They are hands that have built, and fixed, and given so much to the world.

Now, they are giving this.

He is smiling, an unabashed, wide smile that crinkles the corners of his eyes. There is a brightness in them, the shining hint of a tear held in check. It is the look of a man who has reached the goal he has worked for his entire life.

His son, twenty-five and built with the same solid frame, looks at the keys and then at his father. A smile touches his lips, but it is a serious smile. He is quiet, reflective, his father's stoic nature mirrored in him. He feels the immediate rush of happiness, but beneath it, something heavier. He thinks of his own friends, good men, who are just now celebrating their first homes, nervously signing papers that would bind them for thirty years. He thinks of the weight of that, and the profound, absolute lightness of this moment.

A silent vow forms in his mind. *I will not waste this gift.*

He reaches out. His own hands, just beginning to show the marks of his own blue-collar trade, close over the keys. He feels the cold, sharp-edged metal against his palm, and for a second, the warmth of his father's calloused hand.

He meets his father's gaze. In that wordless look, everything is said. The son sees the pride, but he also sees his own future reflected in his father's eyes- a future where, decades from now, he will stand on a porch just like this, passing this same impossible gift to his own child.

They are the first link in a new chain.

The son's grip tightens on the keys. He turns from his father and faces the front door. His door. He puts the key in the lock. It clicks, and the door swings open.

The Miracle Investment

We all know the miracle of compound interest.

You've seen the charts. You know the drill: Invest a little bit of money when you're 20, and you're a millionaire by 65.

The thing about compound interest is that it requires two ingredients: capital (money to invest) and time.

When you're young, you have all the time in the world, but you have no capital.

By the time you're in your peak earning years, you finally have capital, but you've lost the time.

You have no time for it to compound.

It's a catch-22. And it's designed to keep you running in place, always feeling like you're one step behind.

But what if I told you there was a financial product that gave you the best of both worlds? A product that could give you both the high income and the time to invest it?

What if there was a financial product that could look at your entire life's "surplus earning potential"—all the money you're likely to earn over and above your living costs for the next 30 or 40 years—and give you access to it now?

Let's put a number on it. Let's imagine that "surplus potential" for an average, educated, and ambitious person is $800,000. Almost a million. That's the money you'll eventually earn and could (in theory) save over your working life.

Now, this product wouldn't just dump eight-hundred grand in your lap. That would be too perfect, wouldn't it? Instead, what if it started paying it to you in predictable installments starting today?

Let's do the math. Play along at home if you want.

$800,000 spread out over 30 years is just over $26,600 a year.

Divide by 12, and we get $2,222.

Every single month.

Imagine that. An extra two grand landing in your bank account every month, on the first of the month. Rain, hail or shine. For the next 30 years.

But you don't spend it. This isn't for cars or vacations. This is for building.

Indulge me a little more. I'm promising you generational wealth here, remember?

What happens if you take your $2,222 every month and invest it? What if you put it into an index fund and left it alone for 30 years?

Your $2,222, compounding month after month, year after year, at a conservative, predictable rate, let's say 8%.

After 30 years, your $800,000 of "surplus potential" hasn't just been paid to you. It has been transformed.

It would be worth over $3 million.

Okay, maybe it's not quite "generational wealth", but it's a good start, right?

What would you do with $3 million?

No, really. Stop and think about it. Don't brush past this part. Let your mind really go there. What would that number, sitting in your name, really mean?

What would it mean for your kids? Would you pay for their entire college education so they could graduate with zero debt, free to chase any dream? Would you use it to give them the exact same gift we pictured in the opening scene—the keys to their first home, free and clear?

What would it mean for you? What car would you drive? I know what I'd do. I'd buy a Porsche. A red one. I've always wanted a red Porsche. Where would you have your vacation house? A quiet cabin in the woods? A beachfront condo where you can hear the ocean?

Think of the freedom. The ability to say "fuck off" to a boss you hate. The ability to take a year off just to be with your family.

Now, flip it.

Imagine your parents had known this. Imagine they had used this product, and on your 25th birthday, they hadn't just given you a card. They had given you $3 million.

What would your life look like today?

How different would your choices have been? How much less stress would you have carried? How much more freely could you have built the life you wanted, instead of the life you had to settle for?

That's the feeling. That's the power of the number.

I'd fix the water damage in my ceiling. I'd take my wife to Italy. I'd pay off my brother's student debt. There isn't a lot I wouldn't do with $3 million.

Think about it. Feel that number in your gut. An extra two grand a month, auto-invested, turning into $3 million.

I know what you're thinking. It sounds too good to be true. A "secret" product that just gives you your future money now? Paid in monthly instalments that you can invest to build an inheritance worth millions?

It sounds like a magic trick.

But the numbers don't lie. The logic is sound. And that feeling in your gut—the one that says a system this powerful, this logical, must exist in some form—is correct.

This product is very real. In fact, millions, maybe *billions* of people use it every single day.

You've just been taught not to see its true potential.

The Reveal

All right, all right. I've kept you in suspense long enough. The miracle investment that generates compound growth based on your projected future earnings to create millions. You want to know what it is.

Do you want the good news or the bad news first?

Let's start with the good news. You are, in all likelihood, going to earn a surplus of $800,000 over the next 30 years. That part is true.

Now for the bad news.

You already have this "miracle product."

It's your mortgage. And you're on the losing side of the deal.

Let's look at the numbers again so I can prove how much of a sucker the banks are making out of us.

The $800,000 future surplus? That's your total repayment to the bank.

The $2,222 monthly instalments? They are your repayments.

And the $3 million? That's the bank's patience rewarded.

It's not a guess. It's a calculation. In fact, the reason I know you will earn $800,000 over the next 30 years is because the bank wouldn't lend to you otherwise. They've already done the math. It's called a 'serviceability assessment,' and it's the bank's guarantee that you are a safe bet.

And how much did it cost the bank up front to secure their $3 million fortune? What bait did they have to dangle in front of you to make you bite?

It was the $400,000 principle you borrowed to buy your house.

The Miracle Investment: Visualized

We've heard it all before. Compound interest is "the Eighth Wonder of the World." It's "The most powerful force in the universe."

This is true. Compound interest is a miracle.

But a miracle is just a phenomenon. It doesn't have a conscience. It doesn't care if it's making you rich or making someone else rich off your back.

The miracle has two faces. Here they are for comparison. One represents the path we've been told is a smart and mature decision. And one is the true cost of that decision.

BORROWER'S RECEIPT

30 YEARS FROM NOW,

YOU GET: 1 HOUSE

PAYABLE: **$800,000**

BANK'S RECEIPT

30 YEARS FROM NOW,

THEY GET: $3MILLION

PAYABLE: **$400,000**

The Lost Harvest

We've put a number on it. I've proved that the bank turns your $400,000 loan into a $3 million fortune for itself, all on your back.

But you need to stop thinking about it as just a number.

That $3 million isn't just a figure on the bank's ledger. It's a physical, tangible thing. It's your family's harvest. It's a vast, golden field of wheat, grown from 30 years of your life—your work, your stress, your sacrifice.

And just when it's ready to be gathered, the bank arrives. It's the grim reaper in a pinstripe suit, and it carries a scythe. It walks into your field, cuts down your harvest, and hauls it all away, leaving you with nothing but the stubble.

And then it turns to your children and tells them to start planting again.

This is the greatest, most insidious theft of our time. And it's been normalized as "the cost of homeownership." It is a multi-generational crime, and it's time we called it what it is.

Let's talk about the profound injustice of this arrangement.

When you sign those mortgage papers, you are taking on 100% of the risk. You are the one who has to show up to work every day for 30 years, rain or shine, sick or healthy, in a job you love or a job you hate. You are the one who has to endure recessions, layoffs, and inflation. You are the one who feels that cold spike of fear if a paycheck is late. You, and you alone, carry the entire burden of failure. If you miss your payments, you and your family are booted to the curb, your life in ruins.

The bank, on the other hand, takes on zero risk.

They "serviceability test" you to make sure you can afford the payments. They take the house itself as collateral. They've done the math. They literally cannot lose. They've engineered a 30 year contract where you do all the work, take all the risk, and they get all the reward.

It's insidious. And it's time to be angry about it.

That $3 million is your money. It is your family's wealth.

That's your Porsche. Yes, I'm serious. "My fucking Porsche!" you should be shouting. "They took my fucking Porsche!"

And it's more than a car.

It's every family vacation you can't take.

It's every year you spend stuck in a job you hate, chained to your desk by that direct debit.

It's the second-hand car you buy because the budget is too tight for a new one.

It's the constant, grinding, low-level anxiety that thrums beneath your entire life.

It's the fight you have with your wife about the grocery bill. It's the awful, hollow feeling of biting your tongue when she wants to take the kids on a weekend away, because you know it'll have to go on the credit card and you've "already said no too many times" this month.

That feeling is the sound of the reaper's scythe. It's the feeling of your harvest being stolen, stalk by stalk, week by week, for 30 years.

You have been living a life of manufactured scarcity, fighting over scraps, while the bank hauls away your family's fortune by the truckload.

This is the moment of cold, terrible clarity.

You are standing in this plundered field, furious, looking at the $3 million hole in your life. And then you look over, and you see your children. They are playing at the edge of the field, innocent, unaware that The Script of their life is already being written.

And this is the thought that should stop your heart:

Unless I do something now, this same fate awaits my children.

You realize that by accepting this trap, you are not just sacrificing your own life. You are actively building the prison for the next generation. You are teaching your son to pick up the plow and tend the same field, only to have his harvest stolen by the same reaper.

This is the choice.

You can be just another link in the chain. Or you can be the hammer that breaks it.

Right now, that feeling in your gut isn't a plan. It's just energy without an outlet. It is a raw, churning, powerful resolve that something must change.

Hold on to that feeling. It's the most important thing you have.

It is the seed from which your new family tree will grow.

Part II: The Great Unlearning

Century Tree Press

What Else is Behind the Curtain?

You've seen behind the curtain.

The trick is ruined. You can no longer look at a 30 year mortgage as a "rite of passage" or the "key to the middle class." You see it for what it is: a meticulously engineered, multi-generational theft.

You know the scam. You've felt that hot, coiling anger. That raw energy, that resolve that something must change. You're ready to break the chain and build a new legacy for your family.

But that energy, that righteous anger, is not enough. Not yet.

Why? Because the $3 million theft is just the result of the scam. It's not the scam itself.

The real scam is the script that makes the theft possible. It's the system of beliefs, assumptions, and social pressures fed to you since birth, all designed to make you walk into the trap willingly, believing it was your own idea.

To break the chain, you don't just need a new financial plan. You need to unlearn every single rule that has been holding you in place.

To help you see the script in action, I will tell you a story. It's the story of two men, Ben and Adam. Adam is the man who follows the script. He has the big house, the impressive job, the piano, and the crushing debt to match. Ben is the man who is quietly, deliberately, writing his own.

Their journey is the laboratory where we'll dissect every piece of this Great Unlearning.

But I need to give you a serious warning before you turn the page.

The ideas in this section are controversial. They are harder to swallow than what you've read so far. They will challenge everything you've been taught about money, success, career, and even your responsibility to your family. This is not for the tourist. This is not for the faint of heart.

This section is only for those who are truly serious about tearing up the script, no matter the social cost.

If you're ready, let's begin.

Chapter 2

Debt Is Not a Rite of Passage

Scene 1: The Crossroads

Twilight.

The sun had set, but the sky held on to a bruised, fading glow that silhouetted the rooftops. It had been a long day. The breeze was picking up, carrying the first real chill of the evening, and Ben was glad for it.

He stood on the pavement outside his house, flanked by his brother and his father. The visit was over; they were heading home. Ben looked at his own house. An old, overgrown oak tree in the front yard, planted by the original owners decades ago, plunged the lawn into deep shadow. Ben looked at the thickest branch, the one that reached out over the driveway. It would be perfect for a swing.

From every window of his house, warm, yellow light spilled out onto the dark grass. It was a beacon. It was home.

Then, he looked up the hill.

Adam's new house was perfectly visible from here. A large, geometric shadow against the dying light. The last rays of the sun, now gone from the valley, caught the sharp, brand-new roofline, giving the house a strange, sterile halo. It was new. It was impressive. And all its lights were off. A dark, empty box waiting for a life to begin.

His father, standing between them, pulled them both close, draping a heavy arm over each of their shoulders. His arm was around Ben, but his gaze—his entire, beaming focus—was aimed squarely up the hill.

"My sons," his father boomed, his voice thick with a pride that was almost possessive. "The homeowners. Boys, I am so proud of you both."

He gave Adam's shoulder a rough, affectionate shake. "Adam, never in a million years did I think one day a son of mine would be able to afford a house on the hill. Look at that thing. Just look at it."

He then turned his head to Ben, his gaze briefly taking in the smaller, older house. "And Ben. With the baby on the way, it was a sensible move to get a roof over your head. It's a first step."

A first step. The words pricked at Ben, a small, familiar sting. He wanted to be happy, to soak in his father's praise, but the comment made him feel... small. He looked at his father, beaming, and tried to enjoy the moment.

Adam laughed, a sound that was sharp and a little too loud, one that didn't quite reach his eyes. "I'm glad you like it,

Dad," he said, running a hand through his hair. "But with this mortgage... it feels like I'm at the bottom of a mountain."

"Of course it does!" his father roared, clapping Adam on the back so hard he nearly stumbled. "That's how you know you've done something big! I felt the same way when I bought our first place. Everyone does. It's a rite of passage."

A rite of passage.

The words hung in the cooling air. A strange, involuntary image flashed in Ben's mind: a line of men walking willingly into a meat grinder. He blinked, shaking the ugly thought away. *Where did that come from?*

He tried to focus. His father was proud. His brother had a new house. This was a good moment. He *should* be happy for them. But as he stood there, his father's arm heavy on his shoulder, he couldn't shake a rising sense of unease. He looked from his beaming father to his anxious brother, who was already staring at the ground, and something felt profoundly wrong.

They all saw a mountain to be climbed, a "rite of passage" to be endured.

Ben looked at the dark house on the hill, and for the first time, he felt a cold, creeping dread. The pride in his father's voice, the anxiety in his brother's, the sheer size of the "mountain"... it all combined into a single, chilling thought that settled in his stomach.

This doesn't feel like a rite of passage.

It feels like a life sentence.

The thought was so clear and so cold that it seemed to silence the world around him. He felt a sudden need to pull away, to take a step back and breathe, but he stayed put, the weight of his father's arm holding him in place.

His father, lost in his proud reverie, finally gave them both one last squeeze and stepped back, clapping his hands together. "Right. We'd best be off. Adam, you're driving."

Adam nodded, jingling his keys. He turned to Ben. "You sure you don't want to come and have a drink with us?"

Ben shook his head, managing a smile that felt a little more genuine, if still conflicted. "I can't tonight. Early start tomorrow, and I want to see Sarah before she falls asleep."

He needed to get back inside. Back to the warm light.

"Suit yourself," Adam said with a shrug, already walking to the car. "See you next week, brother."

"See you," Ben said.

He watched them get into the car. He raised a hand as they pulled away from the curb, the red tail lights shrinking as they made the turn, heading up the hill.

Ben stood alone on the dark street, his smile fading. He listened until the sound of the engine was gone, replaced by the rustling leaves of the old oak tree above him. The houses on his street were silent. From somewhere down the road, in the dark, he could hear the distant, lonely hum of the crossroads.

Debt Is Not a Rite of Passage

What a romantic idea. What a noble, character-building trial.

Forget surviving in the wilderness, forging a spear, or mastering a difficult trade. The new coming-of-age story is a 45-minute meeting with a mortgage broker. The great crucible of modern adulthood is successfully qualifying for a loan that will bleed you dry for the next three decades.

Ah, yes. The sacred trial of... paperwork. The character-building test of... interest capitalization. The profound spiritual journey of... the 30-year amortization schedule.

We have collectively bought into the delusion that this specific, modern, soul-crushing financial instrument is a noble burden. We've been convinced that this form of servitude is what separates the adults from the children.

It's the great unifying experience! We all gather around the ceremonial bonfire (an Excel spreadsheet of our debts) and compare war stories. "My variable rate just went up." "Oh yeah? Well, my introductory offer just expired." We wear our financial stress like a badge of honor.

We do this because "everyone else is doing it." It's the social script. It's what *you do*. You get the degree, you get the job, you get the car loan, you get the mortgage. Congratulations, you've collected the whole set. You are now a fully participating, responsible member of the economy.

Let's be honest. This isn't *your* rite of passage.

It's the bank's.

It's the celebration they have in their boardroom when you are successfully branded, tagged, and entered into the ledger. It's the moment you are officially converted from a person into an asset. A reliable, 30-year income stream. Your "rite of passage" is their "quarterly earnings."

The script is designed to make you feel trapped. It is a prison with two doors, both of which lead back to the same cell. It presents you with a series of false, pathetic choices, all of which end with you signing your name on the dotted line.

- Get a mortgage, or you will rent forever. (The choice: be a "homeowner" who actually rents from the bank, or be a renter who rents from a landlord. How liberating.)

- Get student debt, or you will be uneducated. (The choice: a lifetime of debt, or a lifetime of low-earning potential. Pick your struggle, peasant.)

- Get a car loan, or you will be immobile. (The choice: pay twice what the car is worth, or give up three hours a day to public transport. What a wonderful menu of options.)

It is a system that always, *always* ends with the same line: "You have no choice but to sign."

But you do.

There is a third way.

Buy a house with your parents' money.

Read that line again. It is designed to be outrageous. It's designed to make you recoil. Your immediate reaction is probably, "That's not an option for me. That's for trust-fund kids. That's ridiculous."

Good. That feeling of outrage is the system protecting itself. It's the knee-jerk defense of the script you've been programmed to follow.

But understand the true meaning. **This blueprint is not about what you can take, but what you can build.**

It is not about *receiving* a handout from your parents. It's about *becoming* the parent who can provide that foundation. It's about fundamentally changing your family's financial trajectory so that your children never have to face that false choice in the first place.

This is what The Old Money Blueprint is all about.

It's the plan to systematically and permanently remove the bank from your family's financial equation. It's how you stop the generational leech. It is how you reclaim the lost harvest—the hundreds of thousands of dollars in interest—so that your children, and their children, can benefit from a lifetime of uninterrupted compounding growth.

It is how you turn their "rite of passage" into your family's liberation.

SKEPTICS CORNER

Q: "This is inspiring and you're right, it feels like a trap. But that 'buy a house with your parents' money' line made me angry. My parents are working class, they can't help me. Is this book just another 'be born rich' philosophy?"

I'm glad you had that reaction. It means you're one of us.

That line is *designed* to make you feel that outrage, because it's the exact point of the book. The blueprint I'm about to show you is not about what your parents can do for you. It's about what you are going to do for your children.

You are not the trust-fund kid in this story. You are the *Pioneer*. You are the first link in a new chain. You're the one who stops the lost harvest and starts the new one. This book isn't for people who are already rich. It's for the people who are going to build a legacy from scratch.

Q: "Okay, I'm the Pioneer. But I'm 32 years old and I already have a $500,000 'life sentence.' The ship has sailed for me, hasn't it? Is it too late to start?"

Absolutely not. In fact, you're in the perfect position. You don't need me to tell you the mortgage is a trap. You feel the weight of it every month already. You have the anger and the motivation that an 18-year-old doesn't.

The Old Money Blueprint is not an all-or-nothing plan. It's a set of tools. It's the blueprint we'll use in Part III to build your Century Tree *while* you're attacking that debt. You're not at the end of your story. You're at the beginning of your *real* mission.

Q: "You've told me I'm in a trap. You've told me the choices I'm given are false. But you still haven't told me what the *actual* alternative is. How am I supposed to save hundreds of thousands in cash?"

You're right. And I'm not going to insult you by saying 'just budget better.'

Part I of this book was the 'why.' It was the red pill. Part II, which we're in now, is about unlearning all the lies the script has taught us.

Part III is the 'how.' It's the step-by-step, practical blueprint-the 'Builder's Waterfall' that shows you exactly how to allocate your capital, build your Fortress Fund, and plant your Century Tree.

You've just woken up from the matrix. Now, I'm going to teach you how to see the code.

Q: "I'm currently renting and saving for my first home. Are you telling me I should keep renting forever? In the real world, I have to get a mortgage to buy a house. What am I supposed to do?"

You're right. We live in the real world, and in the real world, you will almost certainly have to take out a mortgage.

But there is a difference between taking out a mortgage because it's a 'rite of passage' and taking one out because it's a necessary evil.

The first person signs the papers with pride, buys the biggest house the bank will allow, and accepts the 30-year sentence as normal. They are asleep.

The second person—the Pioneer—signs the papers with a sense of grim determination. They buy the most modest house that meets their needs. They know it's a trap. They know they are the bait. And from day one, they have a ferocious, strategic plan to make sure their kids never fall into it.

You have to eat the shit sandwich. But you do it with your eyes wide open, and you finish it as fast as you possibly can.

Chapter 3
The Old Money Myth

Scene 2: The Night Run

The only sound was their feet.

Thud-thud-thud on the pavement, a steady rhythm in the dark.

It was the only time they could get out now, with kids and wives and the endless, crushing weight of mortgages. The evening run was their one shared escape. The path was straight, boring, and dark, running alongside the train line, a concrete scar through the quiet suburbs.

Ben's breathing was already coming in ragged bursts, a sharp stitch forming in his side. Adam, naturally fitter, ran beside him with an easy, infuriating grace, his breath barely catching.

For Adam, these runs were decompression sessions, a place to vent about work, wives, and the general state of things. Ben, as always, was the listener. But tonight, Adam wasn't just decompressing. He was vibrating with a giddy, restless energy.

He let out a short laugh, half-pant, half-giggle.

"Man," he said, "you know I was telling you about my mate? The one with the old money girlfriend?"

Ben just grunted, a short 'hmph' that was half exertion, half acknowledgment. It was all Adam needed.

"We just had a boys weekend at her family's holiday place... and holy *shit.*" Adam's voice cut through the rhythm of their run. "You would not believe it, man."

Ben's curiosity was piqued, stronger than the ache in his lungs. This was it. A glimpse behind the curtain. The "unscripted" half, as he'd started to think of them. The families who operated on a different set of rules, who hadn't been handed the same blueprint as everyone else.

"Okay," Ben managed, the single word costing him a full exhale.

Adam launched in, the words tumbling out. "We stayed in a *settler cottage.* Like, an *actual* settler cottage," he said, the reverence in his voice unmistakable. "This beautiful old brick house, man, right on the beach. And a lawn... bro, it was a whole *acre* of lawn. Just... lawn. A settler cottage!"

Ben thought of his own modest yard. He'd been proud of it; it was large by today's standards, a patch of green he'd fought for, a place for his kids to play. He saw himself as a pioneer in his own right, the first in his line to build something...

Before the thought could even settle, Adam steamrolled on, oblivious.

"This girl's family, way back... they were *original settlers*. For real. There's like ten families now that all share this place, it's all in some massive trust fund, all that shit..."

He shook his head, a dark shape against the occasional passing streetlight.

"Damn, man... how *lucky* is this guy? My mate? He's not even ambitious! He's a total dropkick, honestly. How is it always the dropkicks who just fall into this? Just... luck."

The word hung in the cool night air. *Luck*.

A sudden, deafening roar ripped through the quiet as a train thundered past, a blur of light and noise, shaking the very ground under their feet. For those ten seconds, Ben was alone in the sound, his thoughts suddenly sharp and clear, illuminated by the flash of the carriages.

Ben kept running, his feet striking the pavement. *Thud. Thud. Thud.*

He didn't say what he was thinking. He didn't have the breath, and he knew, deep down, Adam wouldn't get it anyway.

He thought, *Yeah, brother. Just lucky. I guess our wives came from a lottery too, and we just pulled the short straws. Does he really believe that?*

He looked at the dark, unending path ahead. No. It wasn't *luck*. It was a mentality.

He pictured that settler cottage, the brick and the acre of lawn. It didn't just appear. It started with a pioneer. Someone who, generations ago, was *just like him*.

Someone had built that cottage with their bare hands.

And more importantly, someone's son, and his son after him, had the discipline to hold onto it. They'd held it through depressions when selling it would have been easy. They'd held it through world wars when the future was a black hole. They hadn't sold it for a quick profit, hadn't leveraged it to buy a new car, hadn't unlocked the equity to go on a holiday.

It wasn't luck. It was a philosophy. It was a blueprint.

The train's roar faded into the distance. Adam was still talking, his voice re-emerging from the quiet, but Ben wasn't really listening.

He was just running, his ragged breath finding a new, harder rhythm. The rhythm of a man with work to do.

The Old Money Myth

If you think old money is "luck"—about being in the right place at the right time, or being born into the right family—you will never create it.

The "luck" that Adam envied in his friend's family wasn't a lottery ticket. It was a philosophy. It was a blueprint. Luck doesn't build a house that lasts 150 years.

A Pioneer does.

The Pioneer is the one who takes the risk. He's the one who leaves his family and country to settle on new shores. He's the one who bets on himself, rejects the script, and looks crazy from the outside. He is the one who, as Ben realized, built that first settler cottage with his bare hands.

That was his great, foundational act.

But you don't need to sail across an ocean or build a house from stone to become the pioneer of your own bloodline. Your great, foundational act is different. Your great act is the exorcism.

It is the removal of the generational leech. It is the rejection of the modern money script that says you must chain yourself to a 30 year bank loan just to have a roof over your head.

Like the original pioneer, this act has a cost. But your sacrifice isn't a single, heroic moment of risk. It's quieter. It's a chronic, daily, private discipline.

It's the decision to get a smaller mortgage than you can afford. It's driving an older car while your mates get new ones. It is rejecting the "boomer retirement cruise" script your parents followed.

It is the fundamental adoption of a new mindset: **My money is not my own.**

It belongs to my family. It belongs to the future. I am not a consumer. I am a steward.

And this... this will make you feel strange. It will make you feel like an immigrant to a new philosophy. You have left the "old world" of consumer debt to settle the undeveloped territory of your family's future. When your friends are comparing their new cars, you will feel like a foreigner, a "10 pound pom" who is operating on a completely different set of rules.

This feeling is not a sign that you are failing. It's the *proof* that you have succeeded. It's the evidence that you have successfully broken from the script.

Because this is the truth: **To build old money, you need to reject the modern money script.**

I can hear the objections already. "But all the good land is taken!" "The gold has all been found!" "All the truly great ideas are gone!"

Of course. You're right. It's all over. As if new frontiers in artificial intelligence, robotics, and private space flight aren't being settled *this very second*. As if the digital world isn't minting new millionaires every single day.

Let's be clear: we are *always* in the right place at the right time. There is *always* a gold rush happening somewhere. But to strike that kind of instant fortune? That takes massive balls. It takes a once-in-a-generation idea and the courage of a madman. It's not for everyone.

But don't worry.

This blueprint isn't for that.

This plan has been designed for normal people. It's for the father, the mother, the husband, the employee. It's not about a one-in-a-billion "lucky" strike. It is an entirely achievable, methodical process for building a fortress of generational wealth.

In fact, it's the plan I am following myself.

It's called the Three-Generation Plan. And it begins with you.

Generation One: The Pioneer

That's you. Your mission is to perform the exorcism and live like a settler. You reject the script, you endure the social friction, and you achieve two sacred goals. The first is tangible: you buy your child a house, or you contribute so significantly that they begin their life free of the leech. The second is cultural: you instill in them the Old Money Blueprint mindset, so the gift is not squandered.

Generation Two: The Bridge

Your child, having been given this extraordinary gift, now has a new responsibility. They are the bridge. All the capital that would have been burned to service a 30-year mortgage- hundreds of thousands of dollars- is now theirs to command. Their mission is to take that capital and aggressively fund the Century Tree. They build upon the foundation you laid.

Generation Three: The Steward

By the time Generation Three arrives, the plan is in full flight. They, too, are given a home. They have been taught the philosophy. Their primary responsibility is no longer to build, but to protect. They are the guardians. Their job is to "carry the flame"—to hold onto the philosophy that protects the Century Tree from being cut down by a recession, a bad business idea, or a moment of weakness. They are the ones who, like the settler's descendants, simply hold on.

This is what Adam saw as "luck."

It wasn't. It was a plan.

It began with one pioneer who dared to look crazy. It was built by a bridge who turned freedom into wealth. And it was protected by a steward who carried the flame.

The myth is that old money is a birthright. The truth is, it's a blueprint.

SKEPTIC'S CORNER

Q: "But I can barely pay for my Netflix account! How am I supposed to buy my kid a house?"

I hear you. I really do. Life is tough, and for most people, the script is squeezing them so tight they can barely breathe. The idea of saving an extra *dollar*, let alone a house deposit, feels impossible.

If you're reading this book, it's because you feel that squeeze and you're looking for a way out. You want to build something for your family's future.

But let's be logical. This is a game of compounding. Even if your generation only manages to be *slightly* better off than the last—saving an extra $20, $50, $100 a week—you have started the process. The next generation, building on your small foundation, will be in a stronger position.

So what if your 'Three-Generation Plan' takes five generations? Who cares? You *started* it. You put the ball in motion. The first step, even if it's small, is infinitely more powerful than doing nothing.

Be patient. This whole book is the answer to that "how." I'm not just going to tell you *what* to do; I'm going to show you *how* to find the capital.

Q: "But this is just survivor bias! You're only looking at the 'old money' families that made it. What about all the ones who tried and failed?"

Oh, you're right. How silly of me. Because some people failed in the past, you shouldn't even try.

Are you going to let the ghosts of people you've never met convince you to give up before you've even started?

This blueprint isn't a magical charm. It's a plan. It requires discipline and sacrifice. But it's a plan that works. The families who "survived" weren't lucky; they were disciplined. Are you going to be the reason your family *doesn't* have a success story to tell?

Q: "But it's all about networks! Didn't all the billionaires go to the same schools? I'm not in 'the club'."

You're not wrong. Networks matter. But where do you think those networks come from? Do you think they just appear out of thin air?

They are built. They are cultivated. They are the *result* of a plan.

Maybe all the billionaires *did* go to the same schools. If you implement this three-generation plan, maybe *your* grandkids will go to those schools. Maybe your great-grandkid will be the one who has the "unfair advantage" of a network, all because you decided to become the Pioneer today. This blueprint is *how* you build the network. You just have to be patient enough to let it grow.

Q: "Hey, I feel ripped off! I paid for a plan to get rich *today*, not in three generations!"

That's a fair objection. If you're looking for the most authoritative source on building fast, life-changing wealth while you are still young enough to enjoy it, this isn't it. The book you need to read is ***The Millionaire Fastlane* by MJ DeMarco.**

His CENTS framework is brilliant. It's not *easy*, but it is *fast*. It's a blueprint for entrepreneurs who want to build a high-income business, live the high life, and buy the Lamborghini.

This book is not that. This book is a long-term *philosophy*.

This is the blueprint for ensuring that when you build a massive fortune, your kids don't piss it all away. MJ can teach you how to make it fast; I'm teaching you how to *make it last*.

Chapter 4
What Is a Hobby, Really?

Scene 3: The Piano

The kitchen in Adam's house felt less like a home and more like an operating room. It was all sterile white countertops, gleaming stainless steel, and cold, marble floors. Ben stood leaning against an island, holding a tiny, bitter cup of espresso.

He glanced at his own reflection in the blank, dark screen of the enormous smart fridge. Not a single magnet, kid's drawing, or reminder was stuck to it. His own, back in his small house down the hill, was a chaotic collage of Sophie's art, takeaway menus, and unpaid bills. Adam's house, Ben thought for the dozenth time, didn't look lived-in. It looked like a display model.

"This machine wasn't here last month," Ben had said, when Adam's wife, Kate, had made the coffees. Adam had just shrugged, but Ben saw the flicker in his eyes.

The sound of the girls, Sophie and his niece Abbey, was a pleasant background noise of giggling and conspiratorial whispers from the bedroom down the hall. Then a new sound cut through.

A single, hesitant *plink* of a piano key. Followed by a giggle.

Ben took a sip of the espresso. "So," he said, looking at his older brother. "Who's the Mozart in there?"

Adam lit up. He puffed his chest out, but Ben, who had known him his entire life, could see the nervous tension in his shoulders. He was looking for an ally, not just a listener- and Ben knew Kate hadn't been one.

"Oh, that!" Adam said, trying to sound casual. "A piano like that would be wasted on Mozart, mate. That's Abbey's early birthday present."

Ben saw his brother almost vibrating with the need for validation. He saw the genuine, good-hearted impulse and the foolish, scripted action. *Here we go*, Ben thought. He decided to take it easy on him. This wasn't the hill to die on.

He forced a small, supportive smile. "Well, in that case, you'll have to make sure we get front row tickets for her first recital."

Adam's shoulders relaxed. He let out a short, relieved laugh. "Exactly! Right? You've got to nurture the talent."

"So she's been asking for one?" Ben asked, leaning back against the cold counter.

"Well, not exactly," Adam said, running a hand over the shiny new espresso machine. "She saw some kid playing one in a movie... or maybe it was a YouTube video... and just became obsessed with it. You know how kids get. 'I want to play! I want to play!' So, I figured, you strike while the iron's hot, you know? Get her the best, so she's *inspired* to play."

Ben nodded slowly, processing. The inspiration came from a screen, and the solution was a purchase. He looked at his brother, who was now beaming, fully convinced of his own logic.

"So," Ben asked, his voice quiet and practical. "What was the damage?"

Adam's laugh was shorter this time, and forced. He broke eye contact, turning to the espresso machine to wipe down the already spotless chrome.

"Ah, well, that's the best part," he said, his back to Ben. "You'll be glad to know, I got it second-hand. Absolute steal. Must have been... I don't know, a third of the regular cost?"

He kept wiping. Ben didn't say anything. He just leaned against the counter, took a slow, deliberate sip, and waited. The silence stretched, heavier than any question. The only sound was Adam's cloth on the metal.

Finally, Adam stopped. His shoulders slumped. He turned back around, not quite meeting Ben's eyes.

"Five grand," he said in a rush. "Which, I mean, for a piano of that quality, it's basically an investment, right?"

Ben's forced smile faded. The friendly mask dropped. He set his small cup on the marble counter with a quiet, deliberate *click*. He took a step closer, lowering his voice so Kate wouldn't overhear.

"Five grand? Adam, how are you paying for that?" His voice was a sharp whisper. "You told me *last week* on the run that things were getting tight. That the bonus wasn't what you expected." He glanced at the gleaming espresso machine. "And what's with this stupid coffee machine? This thing wasn't here last month, either."

"Don't worry about it," Adam said, his voice pleading. "I moved some investments around and found the cash. And the coffee machine? I had to get it for Kate to soften the blow of the piano."

He leaned in, his eyes earnest and desperate. "But listen, Ben. If you don't invest in your children's interests, isn't that worse? What's our money for if not for our kids?"

Ben looked at his older brother, and all the sharp, practical anger just... deflated.

It was replaced by a profound, familiar pity. Adam wasn't a fool. He was just a man doing his best, following the only script he'd ever been given. The one that said a good father *buys* things for his kids. He was trying so hard to do the right thing, but he didn't know how.

Ben's expression softened. He put a hand on Adam's shoulder.

"You're right," he said quietly, and he gave him a small, sad smile. It was a concession, not an agreement.

He turned and walked the few steps to the sink to rinse his cup. Through the window over the sink, he could see down the hill to his own small house. He could see the roof, faded by the sun, the large, unruly yard, and the old oak tree with the tire swing he'd hung for Sophie.

He let out a quiet, internal laugh. *Look at me*, he thought. *Living in that crappy little box, lecturing my older brother on how to spend his money.*

He turned from the sink, the conversation over. He gave Adam a nod and started walking down the hall, Adam following a few paces behind.

As they reached the doorway of Abbey's bedroom, the girls, who were standing beside a huge, sprawling structure of blankets and pillows, spotted them.

"Ta-daa!" Abbey yelled, beaming, her face flushed with excitement.

It wasn't just a pile of blankets. It was a fortress. Ben could see where Sophie had used the same knots he'd taught her to secure the corners to the bedposts. It was an impressive piece of kid-engineering, built from nothing but imagination and a bit of practical skill.

Adam stared at the homemade fortress. His face lit up with a genuine, un-purchased joy. The exact same look Abbey had.

"Wow!" he yelled, his inner child instantly awoken. "That's amazing!"

He immediately dropped to his hands and knees and crawled inside. "Show me, Abs! Did you build this?"

His voice was muffled from inside the blankets. "It was Sophie's idea!" Abbey yelled, crawling in after him. "But we made it together. I brought all the teddies in!"

Ben stood in the doorway, a hand on Sophie's shoulder. His daughter just looked up at him, a small, satisfied smile on her face. Her work was done.

"We'll leave you to it," Ben said, his voice full of an affection he couldn't have mustered in the kitchen.

He steered Sophie out of the room. As they turned to leave, his gaze flicked to the corner of the bedroom. A dusty guitar was propped against the wall, a school t-shirt and a pair of leggings draped over it like a sad, forgotten coat rack.

He registered it for a second; a five-hundred-dollar ghost of a five-thousand-dollar investment.

Then he and Sophie headed for the front door, leaving the sound of his brother's happy, muffled laughter behind them.

What Is a Hobby, Really?

Ask a modern man what his hobby is, and you'll often see a flicker of apology in his eye.

"Oh, I just... I collect Funko Pops."

"I guess I'm really into Game of Thrones right now."

"I'm a bit of a sneakerhead."

In the modern world, the word "hobby" has become synonymous with "guilty pleasure." It's the polite, socially acceptable term for what is, in reality, a capital-destroying habit. For many men, a hobby is little more than the trivial, consumptive activity their wife "lets" them do. It's the hour they're "allowed" to go to the basement and play with their toys, a permission slip for a bit of harmless, passive sloth.

It's the activity we apologize for, the one we use to "turn our brain off" after a long week. Like Adam in our story, we've come to believe that the hobby is the purchase. We buy the $5,000 piano, the wall of guitars, the video game subscription, or the shelf of collectibles. We perform the act of consumption, and we get a small, fleeting hit of dopamine. But we are not building anything. We are only consuming.

This is a trap. It's a modern invention that short-circuits a deep and powerful human need.

To break free, we must first understand the mechanism that has been hijacked.

The Hijacking of the Progress Principle

Humans are hardwired with what researchers call "The Progress Principle." It's the ancient reward pathway in your brain that releases a little jolt of dopamine when you make tangible progress toward a worthy goal. It's a feeling of satisfaction.

This reward pathway is an evolutionary masterpiece. It's the mechanism that rewarded your ancestors for building a better shelter, sharpening a spear, or successfully growing food. It's the voice in your head that says, "Yes. That was good. Do it again." It's the deep, lasting satisfaction that comes from building, fixing, achieving.

The problem is, our modern consumerist world has learned to manufacture "junk food" for this very pathway.

It's a short circuit.

Why spend six months learning to fix your own car (a difficult, real-world skill) when you can get a hundred tiny dopamine hits from a video game in one night? Why struggle to build a business when you can feel a "sense of progress" by completing a Netflix series or collecting every-colored "rare" item?

Binge-watching a Game of Thrones marathon provides a chemical reward that feels like the one you get from training for a real marathon. Collecting Funko Pops feels like you're building a valuable portfolio.

But you aren't.

The Event vs. The Process

This addiction to the "quick hit" of progress feeds into a destructive mindset that author MJ DeMarco calls confusing "The Event" with "The Process."

Aspiring entrepreneurs are guilty of this. They chase "The Event": they buy the online course, they order the glossy business cards, they rent the office space. They do everything but the actual, grueling "Process" of making sales calls, building a product, and facing rejection. They are addicted to the idea of progress, not the work of it.

This applies perfectly to the modern hobby.

Buying the piano is The Event. It feels like a major step. You've "become a musician." But the "Process" (the daily, frustrating, unglamorous work of practicing scales for an hour) is what actually builds the skill.

The consumptive hobby is all "Event" and no "Process." The act of buying the video game, the act of winning the eBay auction for the collectible, the act of unboxing the sneaker. These are all "Events." They provide a rush.

Perhaps the most ironic and pathetic example of this is the millions of men who relax by watching Primitive Technology videos on YouTube. They sit on their couches, mesmerized, watching another man actually build something from scratch. They get a tiny, vicarious hit of the Progress Principle—a dopamine snack—by watching someone else engage in the "Process," all while they themselves remain perfectly, passively consumptive.

They are a man starving for a steak, trying to survive by sniffing the air outside the restaurant.

It's a lie. And the consequences of falling for it are devastating.

First, you suffer the erosion of your financial capital. You are blowing your children's inheritance on Funko Pops. It's the

$5,000 piano that sits unplayed, the subscription boxes, the endless upgrades. It's the constant, steady drain on your resources that could have been used to build your family's foundation.

Second, and more tragically, you suffer the erosion of your human capital. All those thousands of hours spent consuming could have been spent learning a skill that makes your family stronger, more resilient, and less dependent on the system.

I want to be clear: this isn't an attack on relaxation. I'm not advocating for a joyless life of constant work. But I am taking aim at the behaviors you know are unhealthy. The ones you feel a twinge of guilt about. The ones you justify by calling them a "hobby."

The Old Money Blueprint demands we redefine the term.

The Builder's Hobby

Let's use a new working definition. A **hobby** is the productive activity you choose to spend your time on after all your obligations have been satisfied.

This definition is critical. "Play time with the kids" is not a hobby. It's a sacred obligation of fatherhood. "Date night with your spouse" is not a hobby. It's a non-negotiable obligation of a strong marriage.

I'm talking about the "empty" time. The time you have after the kids are in bed, after you've connected with your partner, after the workday is done.

The modern man fills this time with consumption. The builder fills it with production.

This is "Ancestral Leisure". It's the understanding that your free time is an opportunity. Our grandfathers didn't really have "spare time." After work or on weekends, they were fixing the tractor, mending the fence, or preparing the cellar for winter. And their children were watching, learning, and absorbing the values of self-sufficiency.

A builder's hobby is one that builds real-world capital. It's an expression of identity not through what you buy, but what you do.

Your hobby can follow one of three productive paths:

It Builds Resilience Capital: This is the path of self-sufficiency. It's learning to fix your own car, maintain your own home, grow your own food, or mend your own clothes. These skills don't just make you more resilient. They save your family real money, freeing up capital to destroy your mortgage and build your Century Tree.

It Builds Career Capital: This is the path of upskilling. It's using your evenings to learn to code, get a certification in sales, master public speaking, or learn a high-income trade. This hobby doesn't save you money, it makes you more money by increasing your value in your primary career.

It Builds Legacy Capital: This is the path of stewardship. It's volunteering for a local cause, coaching your kid's sports team, or mastering a craft like woodworking that you can pass down. This path may not have a financial return, but it builds your character, your community, and most importantly, it provides the living curriculum for your children.

When your son sees you spending your Saturday volunteering, or your daughter watches you change the oil on the car, you are teaching them the core values of this blueprint without saying a word. You are modeling a life of production, not consumption.

This is the true power of a hobby. It's the forge where you build your skills, your resilience, and your children's character.

Stop collecting things. Start building capital.

SKEPTICS CORNER

Q: "Are you saying I can't just watch a movie or play a video game to relax? Does everything have to be a side hustle?"

No, I am not. This is not an attack on all forms of relaxation. We're humans, not machines. True leisure—like watching a film with your spouse, playing a board game with your family, reading a great book, or simply sitting in silence—is an essential part of a healthy life.

The distinction is one of intent and default.

Ask yourself: Are you intentionally watching one movie as a planned night of relaxation? Or have you defaulted to a four-hour Netflix binge that leaves you feeling numb and regretful? Are you intentionally playing a video game for 30 minutes to unwind? Or have you defaulted to a

40-hour-a-week habit that drains your time, money, and potential?

The consumptive "hobbies" I'm attacking are the ones that have become compulsions. The "junk food" you've mistaken for a meal. This isn't about turning every minute into a side hustle. It's about auditing your time and asking an honest question: Is this activity truly recharging me, or is it just a short-circuit for the "Progress Principle"? Is it building me up, or just helping me pass the time?

A builder can enjoy a movie. But his default setting is to build.

Q: "What about sport? Isn't that a good hobby?"

First, let's be clear. We are talking about playing sport, not sinking 12 hours every weekend into watching millionaires on TV while you drink yourself into a stupor. Thats's just another form of consumption.

As for playing, it can be. But like everything, you should audit it: what capital is it building?

If it's Resilience Capital—you're training for a marathon, learning a martial art, or building a stronger, healthier body—then yes. You are making yourself a more capable and resilient human.

If it's Legacy Capital—you're coaching your kid's soccer team—then it is one of the noblest hobbies of all.

But if your "hobby" is a five-hour solo golf game every Saturday morning that leaves your wife to manage the household and the kids alone, that's not a hobby. That's a selfish abdication of your obligations.

And now for the harsh truth. If your family, and particularly your wife, doesn't approve of your "hobby," there's a good chance it's because it is not beneficial to the family. It is a drain on the family's resources, time, or emotional energy. It is, by definition, a "consumptive" act, and you are a boy hiding from your duties. You can call me pussywhipped. That's just cope you're using because you know I'm right.

Q: "So I'm supposed to slave away all week at work and then slave away all weekend fixing my car and cleaning my gutters? I live for my weekend! You must be joking."

This is the script of the consumer talking. You've been trained to see "work" as the enemy and "leisure" as the escape.

Let's reframe this: You don't "slave" at work. You are building.

Every single paycheck is a brick in your family's fortress. Every dollar you earn is tangible progress toward your family's long-term vision. You should be getting a dopamine hit from this every single day, because you are on the path to freedom.

Your 9-to-5 is not "getting in a way of your gaming." Your 9-to-5 is the process by which your family will achieve its freedom. The "hobby" that drains your bank account and your time is the only thing getting in the way.

And the work you do on the weekend? That's not "slaving," that's compounding your freedom. Fixing your own car isn't a "chore"; it's a $500 victory that you can immediately deploy against your mortgage. Cleaning your gutters isn't "slaving"; it's protecting a million-dollar asset from water damage.

The builder doesn't "live for the weekend" so he can escape. He lives for the mission, and every single day—weekday or weekend—is an opportunity to build.

Q: "This is all well and good for a 'builder,' but I'm just not handy. I wouldn't know where to start with fixing a car. Are you saying I'm a failure if I just... hire a plumber?"

"I'm not handy" is an excuse. It's the new "I'm bad at math." It's a lazy abdication of your responsibility as a man to be capable.

The problem isn't a lack of talent; it's a lack of will. You live in an age of infinite knowledge. You have AI that can walk you through a project. You have YouTube, where countless "Dads" on the internet will show you, step-by-step, how to fix anything for free.

You don't need to be a master craftsman. You just need to be willing to try.

The real question is, what are you teaching your children with that excuse? When they see you immediately give up and "call a guy" for a simple problem, you are teaching them helplessness. You are training them to be dependent consumers, just like you. Your job as a father is to model resourcefulness.

Q: "Look, it's my money. I work 60 hours a week, and if I want to spend $500 on sneakers, that's my right. You only live once."

No. It is not "your" money.

This is the logic of a selfish brat, not a father. You are not a solo operator. You are the steward of a family's financial future. Every dollar you earn belongs to the family unit and its mission.

Every dollar is a seed. You can either eat that seed now—that fleeting hit from a new pair of sneakers, that expensive bottle of whiskey—or you can plant it. You can plant it in your Century Tree, where it can grow into a harvest for your family. You can use it to buy back your freedom from the bank.

When you "treat yourself" and eat the seed, you are not just stealing from your own potential; you are stealing the entire harvest from your children.

You do only live once. Are you going to spend that one life as a slave to your impulses, or are you going to build a legacy that lasts for a hundred years?

Q: "My entire social life is built on my hobby. My dad and I bond by watching football all Sunday. All my best friends are from my gaming guild. Are you telling me to abandon them?"

This is a tough one, and ultimately, this is your call. The blueprint is a map, not a prison. The closer you can get to the ideal, the better, but even small adjustments make a difference.

Let's audit this honestly. Is the only way you can connect with your father by sitting in passive silence, consuming 10 hours of media? Is the only way you can connect with your friends by consuming digital content?

What if you proposed a change? What if you watched the big game with your dad, and the next weekend, you asked him to come over and help you build a garden bed with your kids? What if you spent one night gaming, and the next night, you organized that same "guild" to volunteer at a local food bank or learn a new skill together?

If your friendships can only survive on a foundation of shared consumption, you need to ask yourself if they are real friendships... or just a shared addiction.

Chapter 5
The Narrative Hijack

Scene 4: The Inheritance Discussion

The pub was quiet. A respectful, post-funeral hush hung in the air, thick as the smell of stale beer and chip-shop ketchup that clung to the dark wood panelling. It was the same smell Ben remembered from his childhood, from the few times his dad had brought them here for a lemonade and a packet of crisps. The nostalgia of it made his throat tighten.

An old friend of their father's, a man with a face like a worn leather boot, gave Adam's shoulder a final, sympathetic squeeze. "He was a good man, boys. Take care of yourselves."

And then he was gone.

It was the first time they had been truly alone all day. The silence stretched, sticky as the table they sat at. Ben looked at his brother, who was staring into the amber of his beer as if searching for an answer at the bottom of the glass. He was struggling.

Ben cleared his throat, trying to find the right words. "You did him proud, Adam," he said quietly. "What you said at the service... about the kids being his real legacy... that was... that was good."

Adam gave a short, jerky nod, but his eyes didn't move. The silence pooled again, heavier this time.

Ben tried a different tack. "You want to know something ridiculous?" he said, a small, sad smile touching his lips. "When I was talking to Dad about his final wishes, you know, getting the paperwork in order... he told me to use some of the money to buy Sophie a grand piano."

That did it. A sound cracked out of Adam, half-laugh, half-sob, and he finally looked up, wiping his eye. "A grand piano?"

"A grand piano," Ben affirmed.

"I'd give you mine," Adam said, a flash of their old banter returning, "but you and Sophie would just use it for a work-bench."

They shared a genuine, tired laugh. The first one of the day. It felt like coming up for air. The laughter faded, and Adam's expression grew serious again. He traced a wet ring on the table with his finger.

"Did... did Dad really say anything else? About how he wanted us to spend our inheritance?"

"Just the normal stuff," Ben said gently. "Regret that he couldn't give us more. He said to spend some of it making memories. But you know how he was. Once we grew up, he never told us what he thought we should do about anything."

"Yep, that's our dad," Adam said, nodding. Then, almost in the same breath, he looked Ben in the eye. "Have you thought about what you'll do with it?"

Ben felt a small, ugly lurch in his gut. How quickly we move on, he thought. He felt a wave of disgust at the sheer practicality of the question, the coldness of it, just hours after they had buried their father.

The disgust was immediately followed by a wave of shame. Because he was a hypocrite.

He *had* thought about it. He'd made his decision a year ago, when Dad first got sick. He couldn't help it. He was a planner, always ten steps ahead. The numbers had run themselves in his head on a long, sleepless night: the inheritance was the final cannonball that would breach the wall. It would clear his mortgage. It would set him free.

He couldn't say that. Not now.

"I've got a few ideas," Ben deflected, "still... still processing it all, to be honest. What about you? What's your plan?"

Adam saw right through him. A hard, knowing look came into his eyes. "What are you 'processing,' Ben? Whether a small happy meal will meet Dad's requirement of 'making memories'?"

The jab hit its mark. Adam knew him. He knew the money was already earmarked for the mortgage.

Ben felt the flush of shame. He tried to parry, to appeal to their shared, practical upbringing. "You should think about doing the same," he offered. "Pay down some of your mortgage. Get ahead."

Adam gave a short, bitter laugh. "Ben, my half will barely make a dent in what I owe. Besides," he said, waving a hand as if dismissing the thought, "You and I have different definitions of 'getting ahead.'"

Ben felt a lecture coming on. He leaned back in his chair and took a sip of his beer, bracing himself.

Adam leaned forward, his voice dropping, taking on the tone of a man explaining an obvious, essential truth.

"As sad as it is, Ben, these times in people's lives are where the wealth transfer occurs. This is how people get into the better areas, the better schools. This is where our kids' futures are built."

He paused, and his voice cracked, just slightly. "It's fine for you to say you're happy where you are. That you and Sarah and Sophie are happy. But Kate is not happy. Abbey is not happy. All her friends are going to the private school next year. That's where they'll build their network for life."

Ben just listened. He'd heard the argument before, a thousand times, from a thousand different people. Keep up. Get the best. Give your kids every advantage. But he'd never heard it like this. Not from his brother. It wasn't an abstract financial strategy; it was a desperate, personal plea. He could suddenly see the immense, crushing pressure Adam was under from his own family, the relentless, unspoken demand to follow the script.

"You need—" Adam started, his eyes searching Ben's, looking for validation.

Ben finished the sentence with him, the old lesson their father had taught them both, now a hollow echo. "—leverage to get anywhere in this world."

"Exactly," Adam said, seizing on the words. "It's what Dad would have wanted."

Ben's mind flashed, unbidden, to that night at the crossroads, years ago. He could hear his father's voice, thick with pride, this time looking out at the ocean. *Never did I think one of my boys would have a home on the coast.*

He felt sick. Because he knew Adam was right. This was what their dad would have wanted. The big house, the visible success, the proof that his sons had "made it." He would never have understood that the price was a heavier set of chains.

Adam nodded, his plan now fully justified in his own mind. He looked down at the table, his decision set in stone.

"When I die," he said, his voice flat and confident, "my kids will do the same thing."

The Narrative Hijack

Does the old advice ever feel… off?

You've heard it your entire life, in a dozen different ways. From your parents, from your teachers, from the well-meaning uncle at a family barbecue.

"You have to get a mortgage. It's a rite of passage."

"Don't worry about the debt, your house is an asset. It's a forced savings plan."

"I worked hard for my money, let me enjoy my retirement. You can do the same when you get there."

It all sounds true enough. It's delivered with the loving confidence of generational wisdom, passed down from a father to his son.

And yet, you feel a nagging discontent. A quiet, cognitive dissonance you can't quite name. When you look at the numbers for your own life—the staggering house prices, the stagnant wages, the sheer, crushing size of the debt required—this "wisdom" doesn't just feel outdated. It feels like a trap.

I'm is here to tell you that your feeling is correct.

That "timeless" financial wisdom you inherited is not timeless at all. It's a manufactured script, barely seventy years old. It's not a map to wealth; it is a set of instructions, written by and for a specific moment in history, designed to benefit the institutions that wrote it.

You feel like you're playing a rigged game because you've been handed the wrong rulebook. You haven't failed the script. The script has failed you.

To break free, you must first understand where it came from.

The "Co-Parent" in the Living Room

For all of biological history, human and animal alike, survival has depended on the lessons passed down from parent to child. This is a self-evident fact. We are biologically predisposed to listen to our elders because, for millennia, their experience was the only map that mattered.

Then, in the flicker of an evolutionary eye, everything changed.

Following the Second World War, your grandparents and parents rode the greatest wave of economic prosperity in human history. For the first time, a single income could buy a home, a car, and a comfortable life. Education was cheap, pensions were generous, and optimism was the default setting.

And into this unprecedented boom came a new voice. It sat in the corner of the living room, and it spoke with compelling, colorful authority.

The television became a "Co-Parent."

As parents grew more prosperous, the TV told them how to spend their money. It showed them what a "successful" life looked like. Doctors on television told them what cigarettes to smoke and what to feed their children. And for the first time, this "Co-Parent" was not a family member with your best interests at heart. It was a corporation. A bank. A mass-media conglomerate.

This new parent began teaching a new financial script.

It was a brilliant, three-part ecosystem of persuasion.

- The Media created the desire: It idolized the big house with the swimming pool, the new car, the boat, the jewellery.

- The Financial Institutions provided the means: "Easy" loans and 30-year mortgages, presented as the obvious, responsible way to get the dream.

- The News provided the justification: The economy was getting better forever. Life improves for every generation. There is no rainy day you need to save for.

This script was not about building resilient wealth. It was about consuming.

We've all seen the proof. Think of the "good silver"—the set of expensive cutlery your parents or grandparents owned, kept in a special box, and used maybe once a year. This was not a tradition of generational wealth; it was an act of aping what the media had presented as "rich." The mortgage for a house you couldn't truly afford became the modern, far more destructive version of the "good silver."

The Golden Tailwind

This new script—consumerism as a virtue, debt as a tool—was adopted so completely for one simple reason: for the Boomer generation, it worked.

They were drafting behind a "Golden Tailwind."

When incomes were growing rapidly every year, debt wasn't a bad thing. When house prices were low and education was nearly free, "just pull yourself up by your bootstraps" was genuinely good advice. They followed the new script from the "Co-Parent," and the unique economic realities of their time validated it.

So, naturally, they passed that script on to you. They passed it on as "generational knowledge," not realizing it was brand new.

Herein lies the friction that defines our generation.

You are being given a 1970s map for a 2020s world.

You are told to "go into the store and ask the manager for a job," in an age of online applications and algorithmic filters. You are told "my pay was only $6 an hour when I was your age," without any acknowledgement of purchasing power.

And most dangerously of all, you are told that a 30-year life sentence of debt is a "rite of passage," just as it was for them.

It doesn't feel right because it isn't right. The Golden Tailwind is gone. That map leads off a cliff.

This is why we must build a new blueprint. It's not about hating our parents. They gave us the best advice they had, advice that was proven true in their own lives.

It's about recognizing with clear eyes that their script has been hijacked. The world has changed, and the "Co-Parent" in our pocket is now a thousand times more dangerous than the one in their living room.

We can no longer copy what our parents did. The world won't teach our children financial sovereignty. That job falls to us. We must reject the old, broken script and deliberately, consciously, teach our children to think differently.

SKEPTICS CORNER

Q: "So what, I'm just supposed to blame my parents? They gave me the best advice they had."

No. This is not about blame. It's about context.

Let's be perfectly clear: Your parents are not the enemy. They are, in many ways, the first victims of the "Narrative Hijack." They passed on the script they were given—a script that, for them, actually worked.

The goal here is to separate the intent (love) from the outcome (a broken script). You can honor your parents' love and sacrifice while simultaneously recognizing that the financial map they gave you is dangerously out of date.It's not about rejecting them; it's about rejecting the script that was sold to them long before you were born.

Q: "Hang on. My parents followed this exact script and they're comfortable. Their house is paid off. How can you say it's 'broken'?"

You're right. It worked... for them.

Their success is the proof of the Golden Tailwind. They were playing the game in an era of cheap assets, rising wages, and low price-to-income ratios.

The script is broken because you're being asked to follow the same map in a totally different world. They took on a small, manageable mortgage in a high-growth economy. You're being encouraged to take on a life-altering 30-year sentence in a stagnant one.

Their map led to a paid-off home. For our generation, that map leads to a life of being a debt-slave.

Q: "This 'narrative hijack' sounds like a conspiracy theory. You're not saying a bunch of guys in a dark room planned this, are you?"

Not at all. The truth is much simpler and, in a way, more obvious.

There was no secret meeting. It was just a convergence of interests.

- The banks want to sell the biggest, longest loans possible.
- The corporations want to sell you a lifetime of stuff to fill the giant houses those loans buy.

- The media makes its money by selling advertising space to those corporations.

The "American Dream" just happens to be the single greatest marketing slogan ever invented to make all three of those industries obscenely wealthy. It's not a conspiracy, it's just a business model. A business model you've been conditioned to see as a "rite of passage."

Q: "My parents worked their tails off. They deserve their retirement and their cruise. Are you saying they shouldn't enjoy it?"

Of course they should enjoy it. They did work hard. This isn't about 'deserving.'

This is about questioning the logic of the script itself.

Let's ask the hard questions. Is a financial script that results in one generation sipping cocktails on a cruise, while their own children are financially drowning—unable to afford childcare for their grandkids—a logical script? Is it a strong script?

Is a family truly "wealthy" if the parents hold a paid-off investment property, while their own son is being bled dry by a mortgage on his own home? All that capital that could be building the family's future is being siphoned off to a bank, month after month.

If you've been paying attention, you should see how illogical this is.

The old script is about individual success. It creates financial orphans.

The new blueprint is about the bloodline. It asks one, simple question: "How do we, as a family, win?"

Chapter 6

A Modern Guide to Arranged Marriages

Scene 5: The Aftermath

The first sound was the sharp clink of glass on glass.

Adam raised his beer bottle to his brother's, the sound echoing for a half-second in the late-night quiet of the kitchen. They were in Ben's house, fifteen years deep into the story. Adam was leaning against the counter by the fridge; Ben was on the opposite counter, a solid, immovable object.

Adam looked up. Dim downlights. He'd never noticed them before.

I've got those in my kitchen, Adam thought. *Did Ben copy that from me?* The thought was bitter, automatic. An old echo from a rivalry that felt a thousand years old.

He took a long pull from his beer, the taste metallic and stale, and looked around. The kitchen was small, but Ben, ever the practical one, had installed storage all the way to the ceiling when he first moved in. It was clean, but not sterile. It was lived-in. The solid wooden benchtops were a map of Ben's life—scratches from a slipped knife, a pale ring from a hot pan, a dark burn mark from a long-forgotten pot. It reminded Adam of an old tree, one of the ones down by the creek, with decades of initials and hearts scratched into the bark.

A heavy silence settled between them, broken only by the low hum of the refrigerator. Adam hadn't wanted to come here, but his feet had just... brought him. He had nowhere else to go.

Ben, of course, let the silence sit. He waited. Finally, he broke it, his voice low and even. "Do you want to talk about what happened?"

The question hit Adam square in the chest, and he felt the pressure rise in his throat. He tried to wave it away. "I don't have time to think about the past," he said, hearing the speed in his own voice. "The past is done. What am I supposed to do now? In the future? How can I afford..."

He stopped, conscious of how he sounded. *Desperate*. He was drowning, but he'd be damned if he pulled his brother under with him. Ben had enough on his plate. He tried to cover, to turn the panic into something practical, something wry.

He let out a short, hollow laugh. "Guess I can always sell the piano, right?"

He risked a glance at Ben. "And don't even think about saying 'I told you so.'"

Ben didn't smile. His eyes were steady, his face unreadable except for a deep, quiet pity. He just absorbed the feeble joke, the frantic energy, the pathetic attempt at a warning. He let it hang in the air and then cut through it all with one, simple question.

"Did she tell you why?"

"She didn't need to." The words came out sharper than Adam intended. "Come on, Ben, even someone as thick as you would have seen we've hated each other for the last few years."

The insult, "thick as you," just evaporated on impact. Ben didn't even flinch, as if he hadn't heard it, or, more likely, knew it wasn't meant for him. It was meant for the universe.

"And Abbey?" Ben asked.

Two words. That's all it took. Adam felt a strange wave of gratitude wash over him. This is why he'd come. No drama, no "oh my god, are you okay?" Just... this. The next step. Ben was his rock, and Adam felt like a man clinging to it in a storm.

"She's at home with Kate," Adam said, his voice finally steady. "They'll stay there until everything's sorted out."

Another long, heavy pause. Adam stared at the scratches on the benchtop. He could feel his brother watching him. He could see the calculations running behind Ben's eyes, the quiet processing.

"I'm worried, Ben," Adam finally whispered, the admission costing him everything. "How can I afford to keep our place...

and get another for myself? I wouldn't mind sleeping in my car, but then... then I'd never get to have Abbey over."

Ben stayed quiet for a long time. When he finally spoke, he sounded almost reluctant, as if he knew his advice had never been welcome before. "You got yourself in a tough spot, didn't you."

It wasn't a question. It was a statement of fact.

Adam laughed, a dry, internal little laugh. *Yes, I deserve this, brother. I've never wanted your advice before, but here I am now, hands out, begging. What kind of man am I?* He could feel the dark spiral starting, the self-loathing coiling in his stomach.

Before it could pull him under, Ben spoke again, cutting him off. "It's about prioritizing now, Adam. You can't have it all anymore."

The words hit him with a mix of relief and disappointment. He knew Ben was right. He'd known it all along, in the car on the way over. But some small, stupid part of him had been holding out hope that Ben, solid, practical Ben, would have some miracle idea. Some magic solution that would save him.

"Prioritize what?" Adam asked, his voice hollow.

"You know what I'm going to say," Ben said.

"So just say it." Adam's voice was getting louder, the old frustration returning. "You're going to say if I want to see Abbey, I need suitable accommodation. If I want her to stay in the same school, I'll need to live nearby. If I want to afford to live nearby..." He couldn't bring himself to say it.

Ben said it for him. "...you need to sell the house, Adam."

There it was. The final, killing blow.

"Dad didn't sell the house when he and Mum split," Adam shot back, a last, desperate bit of resistance.

"And we never saw him!" Ben's voice rose for the first time, not in anger, but in sheer, cold fact. "He left us in that big, empty house. The only way he could afford it was to move an hour away. Is that what you want?"

Adam just stared at him. He knew it was true. It was all true. He'd known it before he'd even parked his car. He just needed to hear it. He just needed something solid to crash against. He hung his head, the fight finally gone, leaving only a vast, cold emptiness.

The refrigerator clicked and went quiet, and the kitchen was plunged into absolute silence.

Ben let him sit in it for a moment, then his voice softened. "You don't need to do anything just yet."

Adam looked up, a flicker of pathetic hope.

"Tomorrow," Ben said, holding his gaze. "Tomorrow, you wake up. You go to work like normal. And you think."

"Think about what?"

"Think about what's more important to Abbey. The big house next to the beach... or her daddy."

A Modern Guide to Arranged Marriages

Let's start by addressing the title.

I need you to suspend your moral outrage for a few minutes. The term 'arranged marriage' conjures images of historical cruelty, of young women treated as property, of loveless dynastic pairings. The script—the one informed by romantic comedies and a culture of radical individualism—has trained you to see this concept as morally repugnant.

I understand. But the script is blinding you to an uncomfortable truth.

For 99% of human history, across almost every culture, marriage was not an individual, romantic choice. It was a **strategic alliance**.

It was the Habsburgs marrying cousins to consolidate a continent. It's the entire, brutal logic of *Game of Thrones*. It is the foundational, economic-transfer logic hidden in your *own* traditions, even if you've forgotten it.

When the minister at the altar asks, "Who gives this woman away?", what do you *think* that means? It's the echo of a time when the answer was a deadly serious, "I, the head of her house, am transferring this asset, this precious link in our bloodline, to your house, in the expectation that our two families will now be a single, stronger entity."

This wasn't about love. It was about *survival*.

These societies understood, in a way we have been forced to forget, that **partner selection is the single most impor-**

tant strategic, financial, and genetic decision a family can make.

One bad link, one bad marriage, and the work of generations is lost. The 'Eternal Flame' is extinguished.

I can hear you now. *"Okay, I see why they did it back then. But times have changed. We don't live in feudalism. Influencing my daughter's choice of partner is a sick, controlling, and creepy idea."*

Is it?

Let me paint you a picture. A wedding. A father, beaming with pride, walks his daughter down the aisle. He is so happy.

He can't see, or has *trained* himself not to see, the faint, black-and-blue bruise on his daughter's eye, expertly covered by makeup. He smiles past the groom's five children from three previous failed relationships, all sitting in the front row. He nods politely at the best man, who is trying to hide his vape cloud by turning his back on the ceremony. He looks at his soon-to-be son-in-law, at the neck tattoos peeking over the crumpled suit, at the sunglasses worn indoors.

And the father is so proud. He is *beaming*.

He hands his daughter over to this man, kisses her on the cheek, and takes his seat. And as he watches them exchange vows, the script is screaming one, triumphant, delusional mantra at him:

"She's an adult, and I have to respect her choices."

This is the single most dangerous lie of modern, passive parenting.

When your child was one year old, you protected them. You put locks on the cabinets and covers on the electrical outlets. You didn't "respect their choice" to drink poison.

When your child was five, you protected them. You held their hand, taught them to look both ways before crossing the street, and told them not to talk to strangers. You didn't "respect their choice" to play in traffic.

When your child was fifteen, you protected them. You (hopefully) monitored their friends, their habits, and their whereabouts, guarding them against the pull of drugs and bad influences.

At what point did you decide your sacred duty to protect your child evaporates? At what point did you decide your *only* job was to "respect choices," even when those choices lead to guaranteed, catastrophic ruin?

Why would you stop your one-year-old from touching a hot stove but gladly applaud as your twenty-one-year-old marries an addict, a degenerate, or a man drowning in a sea of violence and debt?

Now that I've pointed it out, can you see how stupid it is?

The truth is, the script needs you to be passive. It needs you to feed your kids into the machine, to make them cogs in a system of debt and consumerism. This lie—that your responsibility to protect your children ends at age 18—is the *exact reason* you were so disgusted at the title of this chapter. It's the script fighting back.

Before we can build a solution, we must make one final paradigm shift. It is the most important one in this book.

You do not belong to yourself. You belong to your children.

Most readers will nod at that. It feels right. It's the mantra of the provider. But it's only half the equation. The part you've forgotten is the follow-on:

Your children do not belong to you. They belong to your grandchildren.

Your duty as a parent is not, ultimately, to ensure your child's temporary, individual "happiness." Your duty is to act as a steward, to guard your bloodline, and to ensure your child is capable of providing a safe, stable, and prosperous foundation for the *next* generation.

Your job is to protect your grandchildren. And that job starts *before they are even born*.

If that sounds cold, think of Adam. Think of his daughter, Abbey, as she's described in the fable.

Adam's passive choice, his romantic "leap of faith" with a woman who was a clear financial and emotional black hole, didn't just cost *him*. It cost his daughter. It shattered her foundation, put her in a broken home, and reset the family's legacy back to zero. He failed in his duty as a steward.

That is the cost of inaction. That is the price of leaving your lineage to chance.

The Spectrum of Influence

So what's the alternative? You don't want to be the beaming, deluded father, but you don't want to be a tyrant.

The alternative is *Active Influence*.

This isn't a binary choice between "total control" and "total chaos." It is a spectrum of tools. Your job as a parent is to be all three: a Gardener, an Architect, and, if necessary, a Guardian.

0. The Gambler (The Warning)

This is the default mode for 99% of modern parents. This is the beaming father at the wedding. He did nothing, said nothing, and *hoped* for the best. He is a Gambler, and he is betting his entire bloodline, his grandchildren's entire future, on a single, romantic spin of the wheel. This is not a strategy. It is a tragedy.

1. The Gardener (Indirect Influence)

This is the most subtle and powerful form of influence. The Gardener doesn't *tell* the plant where to grow, he curates the environment so it has no choice but to grow toward the sun.

It's not about forcing your child to meet their future husband at the junior tennis club. The odds of that are near zero.

It's about your choice of neighborhood, your choice of schools, your choice of co-curricular activities and social clubs. It's about immersing your child in a "target-rich environment" for a decade or more. Not an environment rich in "husbands," but one rich in *values*.

By ensuring they grow up surrounded by other families who value discipline, hard work, financial literacy, and ambition, you are giving them the greatest gift of all: the "sense." They will instinctively feel what success and stability look like. They will absorb the markers of a good partner by osmosis, making it almost second nature for them to filter out the losers.

2. The Architect (Direct Influence)

This is the next level. The Gardener shapes the world around the child; the Architect shapes the world *inside* the child.

This is you, as a father, making your family's blueprint known. Explicitly and repeatedly. You don't leave it to chance. This is about setting your family's entire moral and performance standard.

You say, "Gambling is for losers." You say, "Every adult should have a driver's license. It's not optional." You state, "Winners try their best every day, not just on race day."

You are building their script for them. You are giving them the critical, logical framework to filter out the walking disasters before they ever get to the front door. They will know, without question, what the "family standard" is, and they will know when someone falls short of it.

3. The Guardian (The Hard Veto)

This is the nuclear deterrent. It is not a tool for preferences. It's a tool for survival.

You do *not* use the Veto because your daughter brings home a trucker instead of a dentist, or an artist instead of an accountant. If that happens, it's an Architect failure, not a Guardian moment. That is a preference, not a threat.

The Veto is reserved for catastrophic, bloodline-ending threats:

- Drug or alcohol addiction.
- Gambling addiction.
- A history of violence or abuse.
- Crippling, unmanageable debt.
- Profound, unfixable character flaws that signal chaos and instability.

You must have a red line. And your children must know, without a shadow of a doubt, where that line is.

The path of The Gardener and The Architect is a lifelong commitment. The path of The Guardian is a last resort. But all three are infinitely preferable to the path of The Gambler.

SKEPTICS CORNER

Q: "This chapter feels like a personal attack. I married for love, and it feels like you're calling me a fool."

I hear you. So did I. And your child will, and should, marry for love too.

This has never been an argument against love. It is an argument for building a foundation that makes a *successful* love possible.

The "beaming father" at the wedding, watching his daughter marry a disaster? He's not a fool because his daughter is in love. He's a fool because he did nothing for 20 years to give her the standards, the sense, and the self-worth to *not* fall in love with a man who will destroy her.

It's not about choosing between love and strategy. It's about being a good enough Architect and Gardener that your child's 'love' is naturally aimed at partners who will build them up, not tear them—and your grandchildren—down.

Q: "This is insane. If I try any of this, my kid will just rebel and hate me."

This is the fear of the Gambler. You are confusing *influence* with *tyranny*.

Rebellion doesn't happen because of high standards, it happens because of hypocrisy and a lack of logic. If you are an Architect who preaches 'no sports betting' while you're two legs into a multi, your child *will* rebel, and they should. Your authority is unearned.

But if you live by the blueprint, if your standards are logical, consistent, and lived-out, you are not a tyrant. You are a credible leader.

The Gardener and Architect paths are not about control; they are about guidance. You are building a script of success for them, so they don't have to learn the hard way, like Adam did.

If you fear rebellion, it's a sign that you need to be a better Architect and start living the blueprint yourself, today.

Q: "I don't trust myself. What if I'm wrong? What if I 'veto' a good person?"

This is the fear of the Guardian. You're worried about misusing the Hard Veto.

Let's be clear: the Veto is not for preferences. We covered this. You *will* be wrong if you try to veto a trucker for not being a dentist. That is an abuse of power.

The Guardian's Veto is reserved only for catastrophic, non-negotiable, 'red line' threats: active addiction, a history of violence, pathological gambling.

Do you really not trust yourself to know if your daughter's new partner is a violent alcoholic? Do you *really* think you'd be wrong to Veto that?

Of course not.

This fear isn't real. It's just the script of passivity trying one last time to keep you on the sidelines. Your job is to protect your bloodline. You know what a mortal threat looks like. Have the courage to act on it

Chapter 7
On Education

Scene 6: Sophie's Second Thoughts

The late afternoon light in the kitchen was that specific Sunday-Grey, a color that promised the impending arrival of Monday. It was a feeling as much as a time of day; the 'Sunday scaries', as Ben's generation had never called it, but Sophie's did.

Ben found his daughter at the kitchen table, the way he'd found her half a dozen times that weekend. Her laptop was open, displaying dense pages of lecture notes. She was staring at them with an intensity that looked more like apprehension than focus, her brow furrowed as she re-read the same paragraph for the tenth time.

He walked past her, the kettle humming as he fixed two cups of tea. He placed one, milk and one sugar, just as she liked it, by her hand and sat down opposite her. He said nothing, simply unwrapped his own hands from the warm mug.

The silence was a comfortable one. Sophie knew he wasn't expecting a conversation and didn't feel the pressure to stop what she was doing. But after a few more minutes, the quiet presence of her father was a welcome excuse to finally look away from the screen.

She let out a long, slow breath and rubbed her eyes.

"Dad, this course," she said, her voice thin. "It's so hard. Everything is new, and there's so much we are expected to remember. It feels like I'm only just scraping by."

Ben resisted the urge to smile. He'd seen her grades. He knew that for Sophie, "scraping by" meant she was scoring a 92 instead of her preferred 95. But he also knew to hear the music, not just the words. She wasn't talking about grades.

"Is it harder than you thought it would be?" he asked.

Sophie shook her head. "No."

Ben waited. He leaned in expectantly, giving her the space to find the rest of the sentence.

"No," she said again, more firmly. "It's just as hard as we knew it would be. I just... I wish sometimes I could have a break. The school will let us defer for 6 months if we need a break, you know."

Ben nodded. This was the second time the "deferral" had come up this weekend, and he knew it was the real reason for their kitchen-table ritual. He still didn't know what was causing it.

"Sophie, is everything alright?" he asked, his voice calm and direct. "If it's not the grades you're worried about, what is it? Did something happen at school?"

Sophie shrank a little, as if his directness had pricked a balloon. She looked down at her tea.

"It's just... I feel a bit bad. I feel like I'm the only one from my old class who's doing this. Like I drew the short straw." She looked up, her eyes finally showing the real source of the frustration. "I saw Abbey's post this morning. She's in Vietnam. She's 'making memories,' and I'm here learning about... cavities and crowns. It just feels..."

"Like you're missing out?"

"Yes! Exactly."

Ben was surprised by that. "Sophie, I didn't know you wanted to go to Asia."

"I don't," she said, almost too quickly. "That's not the point. But to have the option... the freedom. That would be nice."

Freedom.

There it was. The word he had built his entire life around.

Slowly, Ben got up from the table. He walked over to the tall bookshelf in the corner of the adjoining living room, a piece of furniture that was more of an archive than a library. He reached up to the highest, dustiest corner and pulled down a book.

He returned to the table and placed it between them. It was a simple, black leather journal, its cover worn smooth and its edges softened by many years of use.

"The freedom you want, Sophie," he said quietly, "you are earning it now. Abbey will come home sooner or later, and she'll be five steps behind you. You'll be able to take a holiday every year, while Abbey will still be making repayments on hers."

Sophie looked from her father to the book. "What's with the old book?"

"This book," Ben said, placing his hand on the cover, "is our family's blueprint. We've talked about it before, Sophie, and I know you understand. The way most people live is in servitude to a system. They think they are free, but they aren't. I started writing in this old book just before you were born. Look at the first thing I wrote in it."

He opened the journal. The first page was crisp, the ink slightly faded but the handwriting clear and strong. Sophie leaned in to read the five words at the top of the page:

Debt is not a rite of passage.

"I wrote this," Ben said, "the day I got the keys to this house. To remind me that I don't want to feed you into the same system of servitude."

He looked at her, then turned a few pages to a hand-drawn picture: two charts, side-by-side. One showed a line slowly, painfully descending, under the title "Amortization / Loser" The other showed a line that curved gently upwards, then exponentially, under the title "Compound Interest / Winner" Along the top of the page were the words "Choose your adventure".

"Look at this," Ben said, his voice dropping. "This is what debt robs from families. This is the future for Abbey. For your high school friends."

He looked up from the book to meet his daughter's eyes, to make sure she was paying attention.

She was. Her face was still, not giving her thoughts away, but he knew she was thinking, really thinking.

"Freedom, Sophie," he said, tapping the compound interest chart. "Freedom is inherited. It is earned. It is not borrowed from a bank. Your future is bright, Sophie."

He pointed to the "winner" column on the amortization chart. "This is what most people miss out on. But not you. This is the freedom I want to give you."

He closed the journal, but left his hand on its worn leather cover.

The unhappy tension that had settled in Sophie's shoulders all weekend didn't just ease; it seemed to dissolve, as if a physical weight had been lifted. A small, shaky breath escaped her.

It wasn't that the dentistry course was suddenly easy. It wasn't that the 'Sunday scaries' had vanished for good.

It was just... she wasn't flailing anymore. The semester, the exams, and the degree felt... smaller.

Abbey's trip was just a trip. It didn't have a plan. This, the old book, the charts, her dad sitting right here... this was a plan.

She looked from the book to her father's face. He wasn't lecturing her. He was showing her a map.

The future wasn't this big, scary, dark thing she had to face all by herself.

She felt the solid weight of her father's hand resting on the journal, a quiet promise that they were in this together. A new, calm resolve settled over her. She could do this.

On Education

Be honest. After reading that scene with Sophie, does pre-dental study at 18 sound like a good time?

Of course not. It sounds awful.

That feeling right there? That's the script talking.

The script loves to ask your kids that dreamy, useless question: "What would you do if money was no object?"

It's a fantasy. It's a trap. It's a question designed to make them think about "passion" and "self-exploration," all while someone else is quietly sliding the bill for a hundred grand in student debt across the table.

We're builders. We don't deal in fantasies. Let's ask a real question.

"What would you do if you owed someone $3 million?"

Because, as we saw in Part 1, your bloodline does. That's the Lost Harvest the bank is farming from your family. Your mission is to reclaim it.

If you really owed that much money, you wouldn't be signing up for a degree in philosophy or mixed-medium finger painting. You'd find the path with the biggest, fastest return, and you'd get to work.

The Passion Trap vs. The Blueprint

This is the passion trap in action. The script sells your kids a package of lies:

- **The Job Lie:** "Just get any degree, and a 'great job' will be waiting." (A lie.)
- **The Experience Lie:** "College is for partying and 'finding yourself'." (A high-cost, low-value liability.)
- **The Opportunity Lie:** "This giant menu of courses is a world of opportunity." (A lie. It's a minefield of financial traps.)

The Old Money Blueprint is different. We don't build liabilities, we forge assets. Your child's education isn't an "experience", it's a tool.

So, what's the best tool?

Path A: The Family Asset (The No-Brainer)

Do you have a family business? A trade? A plumbing company? An accounting firm? An investment portfolio that needs managing?

Then what the hell are you doing?

Why would you send your kid off to get a $100,000 debt in media studies when you have an asset right here that they could learn to run? This is the real Old Money move. Their education is an apprenticeship. Their job is to learn the ropes of the family business, to protect it, to grow it, and to one day pass it on.

This is old-school. This is how real legacies are built. It's the most logical, powerful, and direct path to fulfilling the mission.

Path B: Forging a New Tool (For the Pioneer)

But what if you don't have that business? What if you're the Pioneer, the one starting from scratch?

This is where strategic education comes in. You guide your child toward a high-income skill: dentistry, engineering, coding, a medical specialty, a high-value trade.

And here's the kicker: You pay for it.

That's right. If you can, you pay for it. This isn't a handout, it's a strategic investment. It's a draft pick. You are investing family capital into a player on your team, and it creates a healthy, powerful obligation.

They're not a lone wolf taking on "free money" from the government. They're a steward. They're part of the team, and their job is to take your investment seriously and deliver a return.

And what if they "hate" it?

Let's just stop there. Does your five-year-old like going to the dentist?

No. They hate it. You make them go. Why?

Because you're the parent, and you know what's good for them. And one day, they'll thank you for it.

This is the same thing.

A child who understands the "why," who knows they're a steward on a mission, won't "hate" it. They'll see it for what it is.

We are building a new Rome from scratch.

This isn't the time for your kid to fly to Hollywood and "try to make it." That's a luxury for the grandkids.

This generation's job is to build the aqueducts.

The "Winner's Circle"

Here's the final benefit.

When you guide your child into a high-skill profession, you are curating their network.

They will make their best friends—maybe even meet their future spouse—in that environment. Their peers will be other people with discipline, a strong work ethic, and ambition. They'll forge bonds that last a lifetime.

This is the Winner's Circle.

This is the ultimate Gardener strategy we talked about. You're surrounding them with other builders, not passion-chasing dreamers.

This is how you forge an asset.

SKEPTICS CORNER

Q: "What if my child's true passion is art or music? Are you telling me to force them into a job they'll hate, just for the money?"

Let's challenge that word, "passion." We need to separate a hobby from a world-class, validated talent.

Does your child just "like" art, or have they been offered a full scholarship to a prestigious art institute? Do they "enjoy" playing sport, or are they being actively scouted by professional teams?

If it's the second one—if their talent is externally validated and presents a clear, high-stakes path to success—then you absolutely should encourage them to explore it. That is a strategic path, just a much riskier one.

But for 99.9% of kids, "passion" is just a hobby. And that's great! Let them be passionate about it... as a hobby. A productive hobby that builds a skill.

The "follow your passion" script has it backward. It tells you to find a job you "love" (that probably pays nothing) and then spend your whole life stressed about money.

The blueprint is simple: Get the high-income skill first. Whether that's running the family business or becoming a dentist. Use that tool to get your family financially free.

Then, you'll have all the time, money, and freedom in the world to pursue your "passion" from a position of strength, not desperation. Passion is the reward for discipline, not a substitute for it.

Q: "This sounds like a ton of pressure to put on a kid. What if I make this huge investment, and they start to struggle or fail? Do I just cut my losses? That seems incredibly harsh."

That's the script of individualism talking. Remember, this isn't a gamble. It's a team mission.

First, you're the Architect. You don't send your kid into a course you know they'll fail. You guide them to a path that is challenging but achievable.

Second, if they start to struggle, you don't blame them, you support them. You're the leader. If your star player pulls a muscle, you don't abandon them. You get them the best physio money can buy.

It's the same here. If your kid is struggling with advanced calculus, you don't let them fend for themselves. You hire the best private tutor you can find. You invest more to protect the primary investment. This is what a good leader does. The script throws kids to the wolves; the Blueprint reinforces the line.

Q: "Okay, I'm the 'Pioneer' starting from scratch. I'm on board with the mission, but I can't afford to write a $100,000 check for my kid's tuition. Does this whole 'Blueprint' just fall apart if I can't pay for it all upfront?"

No, it doesn't. This is where your commitment as the Pioneer is tested.

If you've both decided that $100,000 course is the right strategic tool, then you commit to attacking that debt with them. Or even, for them.

The loan might be in your child's name, but you make it clear: 'That's just paper. This debt is ours. It's a family mission.' Think of it as a perk of sharing your last name.

You are in this together. In Part 3, when we get to the '60/10/30 Split', I'll show you exactly how to integrate this 'education debt' into your plan and destroy it, just like we destroy the mortgage.

Q: "This all sounds great for kids who can become dentists or engineers. But what if my kid just isn't 'academic'? What if they struggle in school and the idea of college is a total non-starter? Does the blueprint just fail for them?"

Definitely not. In fact, you could argue the blueprint is even more important for them, since they might not be able to rely on a high average salary to get ahead.

This is where high-income, blue-collar trades become the priority. Think: electrician, plumber, painter. These are powerful, high-demand skills.

And here's the key: these aren't just jobs. They are infinitely scalable businesses. Your job as the Pioneer is to help your child turn that trade into a business. A plumber who works for a wage is a cog. A plumber who owns the plumbing business, manages a team, and has a fleet of vans is a builder.

Let me be clear: I am not rating these as second-class options. A trade scaled into a family-owned asset is an incredibly powerful way to build your legacy. My personal preference is just to explore the academic path first because of the Winner's Circle effect we talked about. But the mission is the same: forge an asset.

Part III: The Builder's Blueprint

Century Tree Press

Chapter 8

The 60/30/10 Split & The Builder's Waterfall

The old script is in ashes. You've unlearned the lies and embraced a new, more powerful philosophy.

But a philosophy without a plan is just a dream.

Discipline and motivation are good, but they are fleeting. They won't survive the decades-long mission you are about to undertake. A system will. A system is the legacy you can pass down, just as powerful as the money itself. It's the blueprint that outlasts your motivation and ensures the discipline stands the test of time.

This chapter is that system. It is the practical, step-by-step blueprint for allocating every dollar you earn to forge your family's financial freedom.

This is where the builder picks up the tools.

NOTE: The following section discusses specific financial structures for educational purposes only. This is not financial advice. Consult a qualified accountant or legal professional to ensure these strategies are right for you and compliant with local laws before taking action.

The 60/10/30 Split

This is the high-level framework for allocating 100% of your take-home pay. It removes guesswork, enforces discipline, and makes your financial plan predictable.

But before we even start, there is one non-negotiable pre-step:

The Non-Negotiable Match: If your employer offers a 401(k) or equivalent retirement match, you take it. Always. This comes off the top before you calculate anything else. It is a 50-100% return on your money. To ignore it is to set free money on fire.

After you've secured your match, you will divide your remaining take-home pay into three streams:

- **60% (The Essentials):** This stream covers all your everyday expenses.
- **10% (The "Smell the Roses" Fund):** This is your non-negotiable fund for building a life you enjoy.
- **30% (The Builder's Waterfall):** This is your sacred "Future" slice. This is the engine of your entire plan.

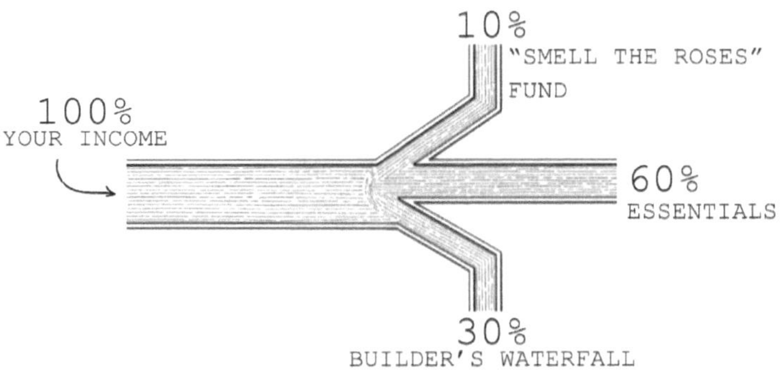

The 60% Essentials Stream

This is your operations budget. It's everything it takes to run your life: your minimum mortgage payment, groceries, utilities, insurance, car payments, and transport costs.

This is also the stream that funds "The Promise". Any minimum payments for your child's student loans become a non-negotiable part of this 60%, just like your own utilities.

The 60% is a target, not a dogma. A dual-income family might live well on 50%. A single-income family in a high-cost area might need 70%. Your mission is to shrink this.

This is your first battlefield. Every dollar you save here is a dollar that can be redeployed into your Waterfall. This is where you get that real, earned dopamine hit from a victory won:

- Call your insurers and get a better deal.
- Switch to a cheaper internet or phone plan.

- Cancel the subscriptions you don't use and choose only one streaming service.
- Limit eating out and bring your lunch to work.
- Use energy-efficient bulbs.
- Buy in bulk at Costco.
- Catch the train instead of paying for parking.

The possibilities are endless. And yes, this might mean facing the elephant in the room: your accommodation. If your location is just too expensive, you need to move. If your Boomer parents have a paid-off investment property that's part of your inheritance anyway, it's time to have a strategic conversation. Why pay thousands to a landlord or a bank when you could be building the family's legacy? I'll talk more about this later.

The 10% "Smell the Roses" Fund

This is the most strategically important 10% in your budget. It's non-negotiable and must be spent.

This is not the "we're too tired to cook so let's get pizza" fund. That comes from your 60% Essentials. This is your planned, intentional memory-building fund.

This is the $500 weekend camping trip. This is the trip to the movies to celebrate a great school report. This is the six-hour drive to the mountains for a weekend in the snow that your kids will still talk about 20 years later.

Don't skip this. You can't have your children remember their upbringing as one of joyless deprivation and then expect them to carry the flame. This fund protects the philosophy. It ensures your family remembers the joy of the journey, not just the sacrifice.

The 30% Builder's Waterfall

This is your sacred "Future" slice. This is the engine. It's a prioritized cascade of money that funds two separate, critical goals: The Fortress and The Century Tree.

The "Why": Fortress vs. Century Tree

To understand the waterfall, you must understand its two goals.

- **The Fortress**: This is your personal security. It's your safety net, your emergency fund, and your own retirement (your 401(k), your private investments). It's the wall you build to protect your family and your mission from the inevitable storms of life.

- **The Century Tree:** This is the untouchable legacy. This is the fund for the next generation. This is your Roth IRA, or your country's equivalent tax-advantaged retirement account. This is the "lost harvest" you are reclaiming.

FORTRESS FUND

- PAID OFF HOME
- EMERGENCY FUND
- 401(K)

CENTURY TREE

- ROTH IRAS
- GIFTED HOME

YOU BUILD THE FORTRESS SO YOU NEVER HAVE TO TOUCH THE TREE

These two goals are separate for a reason. You must internalize this rule:

You build the Fortress so you never have to touch the Tree.

Your Fortress allows you to retire. It allows you to weather a job loss or a medical emergency. It is the selfish, necessary act of self-preservation that makes the unselfish act of legacy possible.

The "How": The Builder's Waterfall in Action

The 30% Builder's Waterfall is a series of cascading steps. You fill one bucket, and the overflow automatically fills the next. You must follow this priority.

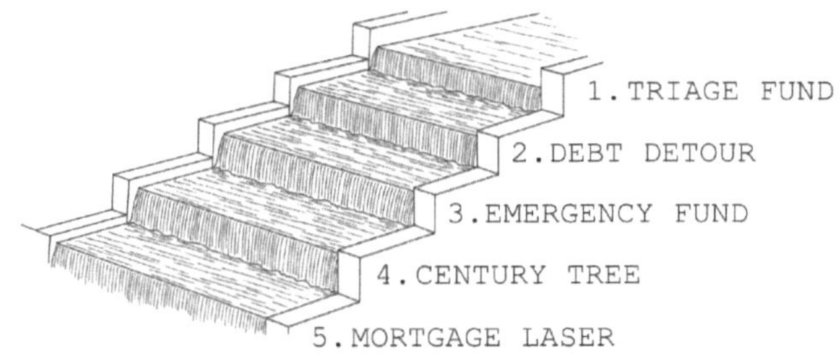

Phase 1: Building the Foundation

Priority 1: The Triage Fund

Action: Your 30% "Future" stream is directed here until you have saved 1 month of essential living expenses.

Why: This is your Fortress's first small wall. It's the breathing room that stops a flat tire from becoming a credit card disaster. This money must be liquid: a high-interest savings account (HISA), a mortgage offset, or even cash under the mattress.

Priority 2: The Debt Detour

Action: Once your 1-month fund is full, the entire 30% stream becomes a laser aimed at all high-interest, non-mortgage debt. This is the parasite on your mission. It is the leech drinking your family's future. You must kill it with ferocious, single-minded intensity. Attack it from the highest interest rate down.

Goal: This is the "exorcism." You can't build a legacy while while you are being bled dry by credit cards and car loans.

Priority 3: Emergency Fund (The "Fortress Wall")

Action: The debt is gone. Now, your 30% stream returns to your emergency fund and does not stop until it is built up to a full 3-6 months of essential expenses.

Goal: Your Fortress is now taking shape. You can survive a job loss, a major repair, or a health crisis without panicking or touching your investments.

The Refill Rule: The emergency fund is your first line of defense. If you use it for a car repair or medical bill, it must be refilled. If your fund drops below the 1-month Triage level, refilling it becomes Priority 1 again, pausing everything else.

Priority 4: Plant the Century Tree

Action: With your 3-6 month emergency fund full, your 30% stream's first job is to max out your Roth IRAs, or your country's equivalent tax-advantaged retirement account. This includes one for you and one for your spouse.

Goal: This is the seed for your Century Tree. This is the untouchable, tax-free nest egg that will compound for decades.

Priority 5: The Mortgage Laser

Action: After your Roth IRAs are maxed out for the year, all remaining funds in your 30% stream are aimed directly at your mortgage principal.

Goal: This is the long, hard slog. This is the siege. But it's infinitely shorter than making the minimum payments. Every extra payment is another brick in your Fortress wall. It is a tangible victory, a strike against the life sentence, reclaiming your family's future one payment at a time.

The Unbreakable Income Mandate

There is a logical "if" in this plan. What if you run the numbers and your 30% future stream is just a 5% trickle? What if you're battling just to fill your Triage Fund, and the idea of maxing out your IRAs feels like a joke?

Then the blueprint is clear. You don't have a saving problem. You have an income problem.

Sorry, but that's how it is. How did you think you were going to build a fortune? By pulling it out of thin air? No. Your mission is clear. You must increase your income.

If you are a white-collar professional, your career is your focus. Get the certification. Chase the promotion. Become so valuable they have to pay you more. If you are blue-collar, read MJ DeMarco. Learn about "value-skew" and "productocracy". Turn your trade into a business. This isn't an excuse. It's reality. That's just how it's done.

Phase 2: The Supercharge

This phase begins at the liberation moment—the day your mortgage is paid off.

Your Mortgage Laser money is now a free agent. This capital is now free to be deployed. You keep maxing out your own Roth IRAs (Priority 4), but the spare cashflow has new targets. You will assess the health of your Fortress and the needs of your family, and you will strategically pivot. Your laser money can now be aimed at:

Finishing Your Fortress: Maxing out your own 401(k) to its annual limit and investing privately, or

Building the Next Legacy: Deploying that capital to help the next generation.

- Funding their Roth IRAs.
- Attacking their mortgage.
- Building a down payment for their first home.

Phase 3: The Legacy

This is the end-game: retirement.

Because you followed the plan, you now live off your Fortress (your 401k and private investments). This allows your Century Tree (your Roth IRAs) to be passed on, untouched.

From this position of strength, you can now strategically deploy the Tree to liberate the next generation, either by drawing 5% a year to pay down your child's mortgage (while the tree still grows), or by providing a lump sum. We'll talk about wealth transfer next.

SKEPTICS CORNER

Q: "A 30% savings rate seems impossible on an average salary. Is this plan only for high-earners?"

No. It's a plan for builders. If your 30% "Future" stream is just a 5% trickle and you cannot max out the Roth IRAs to plant your Century Tree, the blueprint doesn't break. It just gives you a new, non-negotiable priority: increase your income. Use the productive "hobby" time we talked about in Chapter 4 to build a skill that pays. The plan doesn't care about your excuses; it just shows you the next step.

Q: "Your 'waterfall' still prioritizes paying off the mortgage. Why not just pay the minimum and invest the 'Mortgage Laser' money in the market for a 2-3% better return?"

This is the logic of the spreadsheet, not a builder. Remember, we are not playing to win over a single lifetime. We are building a system that is resilient for centuries. A builder doesn't risk his family's home for a few extra points. The market is unpredictable. Black swan events happen. Paying off your mortgage is a guaranteed, risk-free return. It is the act of building your Fortress. It's the liberation of your single greatest expense, which frees up the capital that will build your real wealth.

Chapter 9

The Bank of Mom and Dad: A Strategic Guide to Wealth Transfer

At the start of the book, I painted a picture. You saw the "Builder's Son" on his porch, keys in hand, facing a future of freedom. A life without the 30-year sentence. A life built on a foundation of rock.

You've unlearned the lies. You've torn up the script. At this point, you will have spent years or decades following the 60/10/30 Split and the Builder's Waterfall. Your Fortress will be built, and you will have patiently and relentlessly nurtured your Century Tree.

Now, it's your turn to stand on that porch. It's your turn to create that moment.

But how you do it matters.

This is the "Godfather" chapter. It's not about spoiling your children and it's not about handouts. It's about a strategic, surgical, and permanent transfer of capital designed to do one thing: liberate your bloodline from the life sentence of debt.

The goal is *Liberation*, not Luxury.

In this chapter, I'll show you the tools for this mission. While an overflowing Fortress is a powerful and flexible tool, the asset we'll discuss is the one forged for this exact purpose: The Century Tree. This is the untouchable, generational fund you built so that your children would never have to.

Here is how you deploy it.

The "Slow Drip": The Killer Compounder

The first strategy can begin long before your own mortgage is paid off. The moment your child has any form of earned income (even from a part-time teenage job), you can open a Roth IRA (or your country's equivalent) in their name.

Then, you gift them the money to max it out every single year.

This is the ultimate long-term play. Think about it: you are starting their Century Tree at age 16 instead of 36. That is twenty extra years of tax-free, uninterrupted compounding.

Now, my personal preference is to always destroy the mortgage first before diverting capital elsewhere. A paid-off home is a guaranteed return and the cornerstone of your Fortress.

However, some Pioneers may decide that the compounding power of their child's IRA is a mathematically better investment. I will not begrudge them that choice, as long as one sacred rule is followed:

You never, ever, under any circumstances, touch the Century Tree to pay for your own Fortress.

That Tree is not your money. It belongs to the future.

The Grim Wait vs. The Living Liberation

Let's talk about the ugliest secret of the script: the inheritance.

In the old, broken model, "inheritance" is a polite word for "waiting for your parents to die."

It creates a quiet, toxic dynamic. The children, crushed by their own 30-year sentences, look at their parents' paid-off home and can't help but think of it as "their" future money. Every "boomer retirement cruise", every new car, every expensive dinner is a source of resentment. "They're spending my inheritance."

It's a grim, silent death-watch. The script turns a family into competitors, all waiting for a loved one to die so their own lives can finally begin.

The Old Money Blueprint severs this toxic link completely. We do not leave an inheritance. We give a liberation.

By transferring this capital during your lifetime—by performing the "Liberation Event" when your kids are in their twenties or thirties—you change the entire dynamic. You give them the capital when they actually need it, not when they're 60 and retired themselves.

Your children aren't waiting for you to die; they are profoundly grateful that you are alive. Your relationship isn't based on a morbid financial transaction, but on a shared mission, mutual respect, and profound gratitude. You aren't the dragon hoarding gold; you're the Pioneer who is handing them the map and the tools. This, as much as the money, is the true legacy.

The "Liberation Event": The Main Attack

This is the moment you worked for. You are at retirement age. Your Fortress is built, and you can live off its proceeds. You can now access your Century Tree (your Roth IRAs) completely tax-free.

You have two primary options for liberating your child, who is now likely in their twenties or thirties and has their own mortgage.

Option 1: The Lump Sum (The "Why" Power)

This is the ultimate fulfillment of the mission. You call your son or daughter, you get their mortgage payout figure, and you kill it in one shot. You hand them the keys to their life, free and clear, just as we pictured in Chapter 1. The power of this moment cannot be overstated. It is the "why" made real.

Option 2: The Slow Squeeze (The "Math" Power)

This is the mathematically superior choice. Let's say your Century Tree is growing at 8% per year, and your child's mortgage rate is 5%. Instead of pulling a huge $500,000 chunk out of your Tree, you "squeeze" it. You pull 5% of the Tree's value each year and apply it to their mortgage. The Tree continues to outgrow the debt, you systematically destroy their mortgage, and the legacy fund remains largely intact.

The choice is yours. The Lump Sum has more emotional power; the Slow Squeeze has more financial power. Both achieve the mission.

The Protection Plan: "How Old Money Families Operate"

Giving your child five hundred grand or more is not a simple act. It could be a catastrophic mistake if not done strategically. It's not about trusting your child; it is about protecting the family's capital from a world of chaos, bad luck, and bad partners.

This is where we move from being a "parent" to being a "steward." The most powerful way to do this is to structure the transfer as a formal, low-interest loan.

This single move provides two massive advantages.

Strategy 1: The "Literal Bank of Mom & Dad"

This is the 'Lost Harvest' formula from Part I, but reclaimed for your own bloodline.

Here is how it works:

- You loan your child the $500,000 principal for their home.
- They make their "mortgage" payments back to you instead of to a bank.
- You don't keep the money. You invest 100% of their payments into the Century Tree... for their children

(your grandchildren).

You are basically acting as the bank and force-funding your grandchildren's legacy. You are mechanically installing the blueprint for the next generation. It is a perfect, self-perpetuating system.

Strategy 2: The "Family Policy" (The 'Divorce Shield')

The second reason for a loan is the one nobody wants to talk about. What if your child's marriage fails?

If you gift them five hundred grand, that capital is often considered a "shared marital asset". In a separation, half of your family's Century Tree could walk out the door forever.

A formal loan changes this. The loan is an asset that belongs to you (or to the family trust). It isn't a shared asset to be divided. The "loan" can be structured to be paid back only if the house is ever sold.

How do you frame this without sounding like you don't trust your new son- or daughter-in-law?

You make it a policy. You say, "This isn't personal. It's not about trust. This is just how our family operates to protect the Century Tree for your children and their children. We are doing this for all our kids. It's just a piece of paper that protects the legacy."

It is not an accusation. It is a non-negotiable family policy.

The End-Game: The Trust (The Advanced Move)

As your family's wealth grows, the final move for a Pioneer is to create a formal trust.

This is the ultimate act of stewardship. A trust is a legal entity that "enshrines the Century Tree" and gives it a mission and a constitution. It legally ensures that the blueprint's values are carried out long after you are gone. It can stipulate that the funds are only for a home, an education, or a business—not a luxury car.

But there's a crucial difference here. The "gold rush" trusts of old were passive holding tanks. Our "Builder's Trust" is an active, contributory system, especially in the early generations.

The Century Tree itself is also collective. It is not just your Roth IRA. It is the sum of your IRA, your child's IRA (which you funded), and their children's after them.

This is an advanced, end-game move. It's not something you do the day you finish this book. It's what you do when your own mortgage is gone, your children are liberated, and you have a clear view of the legacy you are protecting.

Disclaimer: You must speak to a trust and estate lawyer to do this. This is not financial advice; it is a strategic philosophy.

How powerful can this become?

Let's imagine your collective Century Tree reaches $12.5 million, maybe in your lifetime, maybe not. At an 8% average annual growth, that Tree generates $1 million per year. This means your family can buy a $2 million home for a new heir every two years, using only the growth, while the principal $12.5 million Tree remains untouched, ready to grow and do it all over again.

That is the power of the blueprint. That is the unbroken chain.

SKEPTICS CORNER

Q: "This is the 'trust-fund baby' problem. Won't giving my kid all this money just make them lazy, unmotivated, and entitled? Isn't the struggle what builds character?"

This is the most common fear, and it's a valid one. But it confuses "giving money" with *passing on a legacy.*

The "trust-fund baby" is the result of a philosophical failure, not a financial one. It's what happens when parents give their kids money but not a mission.

The Old Money Blueprint is the antidote to entitlement.

First, Liberation is not Luxury. The mission isn't to buy your kids a Ferrari. It's to buy them freedom from the bank, so they can begin their own mission sooner and more powerfully. Let's be crystal clear: this blueprint is designed to pay for their education and their home. If your child wants food to eat, furniture for their (paid-off) house, or a car to drive, they still need to work. We are removing their chains, not their responsibilities.

Second, the philosophy is the inheritance. Your child, like Sophie in our story, has been raised on this blueprint. They've seen your work. They've been taught the value of production over consumption. They are not a "trust-fund baby"; they are the "Bridge".

Lastly, the "Literal Bank of Mum & Dad" model builds character. Your child is still required to work, to be disciplined, and to make their "payments". The difference is, their work isn't being siphoned off to a bank's shareholders. It is being captured and compounded for their own children.

You aren't removing the struggle. You're simply ensuring that their struggle builds something that lasts forever.

Chapter 10
The Generational Accelerator

Scene 7: The Young Granddaughter

The late morning sun was high and warm, but a gentle wind kept the heat soft.

The backyard was a perfect, quiet picture. The old oak tree, once unruly, was now a strong, confident canopy. The lawn, once a patch of grass, was pristine. And the fruit trees Sophie remembered planting with her father—stick-like saplings in her memory—were now mature, their branches heavy with the promise of a summer harvest.

From the shade of the porch, Sophie watched.

Her father, a man in his early fifties but with the easy energy of someone twenty years younger, was on his hands and knees in the grass. He wasn't "watching" his granddaughter; he was playing with her, the two of them crawling in a slow-motion chase.

The baby, squealing with delight, made a break for the tire swing.

It was the same swing. The one from Sophie's own childhood, the rope thick and a little frayed, the rubber worn smooth. Her daughter reached up, grabbed the familiar, weathered tire, and pulled herself to her feet, balancing unsteadily.

Ben sat back on his heels, laughing, not hovering, just... present.

Sophie felt a profound, quiet peace settle over her. She looked at her daughter, standing where she had stood, and felt the past and future connect.

A small pang of sadness flickered through her. Her cousin was supposed to be here. Abbey had texted that morning. 'Can't make it, so sorry! Had to pick up a shift.'

Had to.

Sophie thought of her cousin, bright, funny Abbey, now in her late twenties, trapped in a cycle of rent and weekend work. She felt a quiet, sisterly lament. With things the way they were, Abbey was unlikely to have a child of her own anytime soon.

The baby on the lawn let go of the swing and plopped back onto the grass. Ben clapped, as if it were the greatest achievement in the world.

Sophie looked at her father, vibrant and strong, playing with his grandchild in the prime of his life. She looked at her daughter, starting her life on a foundation of absolute security. This, she thought, was the freedom he had built for them all.

The Generational Accelerator

Now for maybe the most counter-intuitive accelerator in the entire blueprint: Have kids young.

I can hear the script screaming back at you already. 'Wait, what? Aren't kids ludicrously expensive?' 'Shouldn't I wait until my career is established?' 'I need to get my own house paid off first!'

That's the logic of the lone-wolf provider, trapped in the old script. The builder, the Pioneer, sees it differently.

The modern "passion" script tells you to spend your twenties "finding yourself." The blueprint understands that your twenties are your years of peak energy, peak resilience, and peak sacrifice. Besides, you'll learn more about yourself raising a kid than you would smoking bongs and getting so drunk you piss the bed.

The mathematical power of the Old Money Blueprint is unlocked by shortening the "cycle time" between generations.

Think of it this way. A century is always 100 years long.

- If your family has kids at age 35, you get three generations in a century.
- If your family has kids at age 25, you get four generations in a century.

You have just given your bloodline an entire extra generation to build, to compound, and to win. It's not just about starting one retirement account earlier; it's about having more generations alive and compounding wealth at the very same time.

The 50-Year-Old Grandfather: A Hypothetical

Let's make this real. Imagine you follow the blueprint and have your child, Sophie, at age 25.

You spend your late twenties and thirties following the 60/10/30 Waterfall. You're attacking your modest mortgage and building your Fortress. It's a grind, but your energy is high.

Now, imagine Sophie, raised on this blueprint, also has her child at age 25.

You are now 50 years old.

What does your life look like?

You are a young grandfather, just like Ben in our parable. You are vibrant, energetic, and at the absolute peak of your financial power. Your mortgage is likely gone, or very close to it. Your "Mortgage Laser" is now a free agent of capital.

Now look at the team you've built:

You (The 50-year-old Pioneer): You are now the "Literal Bank of Mum & Dad". You've already funded Sophie's Strategic Education. Now, you can help her buy her first home, liberating her from the 30-year sentence before it even begins.

Sophie (The 25-year-old Bridge): She is a high-income earner with no life sentence of debt. Does she feel "ready" to have a child? Yes! She feels secure, supported, and optimistic about the future.

Your Grandchild (The Newborn Steward): Because Sophie is liberated, she doesn't have to wait. She can immediately begin funding her own child's Century Tree.

That's it. That's the accelerator. At age 50, you are presiding over a family with three generations of the blueprint in full, active motion.

This is the difference. You aren't on some cruise somewhere, paid for by your investment properties, laughing to your fellow cruisers about how "kids these days don't know the meaning of hard work"... all while your own kid is working a Saturday just to make rent.

Which of these two patriarchs is more likely to build a strong family? Which one is giving their children the optimism and security to start their own families?

This right here is the remedy for the lack of optimism that defines the modern world. When you, the Pioneer, commit to this plan, you are not just building wealth. You are manufacturing the one thing your children need to start their own families: confidence.

You are proving that they are not alone, that they are part of a team.

This is what gives a 25-year-old the freedom and the security to say, "Yes, I'm ready. Let's start our family." And you, in turn, get the ultimate reward. You are not a distant, aging figure; you are a young, powerful, and active grandparent, with decades ahead of you to teach, mentor, and watch your legacy grow.

What's the point of generational wealth otherwise?

SKEPTICS CORNER

Q: "This makes no sense. Kids are incredibly expensive! How can having them earlier possibly be a financial advantage?"

This is a fallacy. Kids cost the same amount of money whether you have them in your twenties or your thirties. The "cost" isn't the variable.

The real issue isn't the price of the diapers; it's the stress.

It's the mental load of that cost plus the mortgage and student debt that the script made you sign up for. That is the real cause of stress, not a baby.

The Old Money Blueprint is the antidote to that stress. It reframes the child from a "cost" into the *mission*. It gives you a plan, a team, and a purpose, which is a far more powerful and optimistic way to live than being a lone wolf drowning in debt.

Q: "I want my partner to have a great career. If we have kids in our 20s, won't that permanently damage their career potential? Shouldn't we wait until we're both 'established' in our 30s?"

This is a good strategic question, but it's looking at the timeline backward.

What's worse?

- Taking a career break at 35, at the absolute peak of your earning potential, and then trying to fight your way back into a senior role after five years away?

- Or, taking that break in your early twenties, before the career rocket ship has even taken off?

The blueprint argues for the second. Front-load the "pause." Get the hard work of raising young children done during your years of peak energy. Build your home, mature as a person, and then, in your late twenties or early thirties, you are free to pursue a 30-year, uninterrupted career, all the way to retirement.

It's strategically smarter.

Q: "This all sounds logical, but I just don't feel ready. I want to enjoy my twenties and 'find myself'."

Let's be honest. You will never "feel" 100% ready. "Ready" is a fantasy. It's the script telling you to chase a feeling instead of building a foundation.

That decade of "finding yourself" is a luxury. And it has a cost.

Every year you delay your mission to "have fun," you are adding weight to your children's backs. You are shortening their timeline. You are making it harder for them to achieve the mission.

The builder understands that "finding yourself" isn't something you do on a beach in Vietnam. You find yourself in the act of building, in the service of your family, and in the forge of responsibility.

Q: "How can I possibly do this? Your whole plan in Chapter 12 is about running a 'Mortgage Laser' with my '30% Waterfall'. Won't having kids just destroy that plan and delay my own freedom?"

It might. It might not.

It *will* be hard. Your income might be stretched thin at the beginning. Your "Mortgage Laser" might slow to a trickle for a few years.

But that's not the point. Ask yourself: Why are you doing this?

Are you doing this just to get personally rich? Or are you doing this to build a bloodline?

It's more important to have a next generation than it is to be rich. Focus on the kids first. The mortgage can wait a few more years. The freedom will come, but the mission comes first.

Chapter 11
When the Storm Hits

Scene 8: The Setback

The piano took up most of the room.

It was the same one, the $5,000 ghost of Adam's former life, its pristine, gloss-black finish still holding a showroom sheen. It was wedged into the living room of his modest, post-divorce home, a gleaming monument that forced the couch and television into a small, awkward corner.

Ben sat on that couch, nursing his beer, and listened to the two competing sounds in the room. In the background, a sports game murmured from the TV, the hyper-animated voice of an announcer cutting through the quiet. In the foreground, a sweeter sound: his granddaughter, Zoe, was at the piano with her cousin. Abbey, her voice smooth and sweet, was patiently guiding Zoe's tiny finger.

Plink. Plink. Twinkle, twinkle...

Ben internally noted the irony of the room. The house itself was old, with the charm of thick wooden floorboards and a cozy fireplace, but Adam had filled it with his own taste: angular, ultra-modern art, stainless steel, and chrome. It was jarring, but Ben had long since gotten used to his brother's ways.

Adam, beside him, was optimistic, vibrant. "The promotion to director is a done deal," he was saying, leaning forward. "Finally. It's about time they saw it. I'm feeling good about the future, Ben. Really good."

He clapped Ben on the knee and took a drink. "So, how's work for you?"

Ben watched his brother for a beat, then looked back at the TV. "I was laid off," he said, his voice even. "Three weeks ago."

The room went silent. The plinking from the piano stopped. The only sound was the distant, frantic yelling of the sports announcer.

Adam was completely still, his beer halfway to his lips. He slowly lowered it, his face pale.

"Shit," he breathed.

He stared at Ben, his optimism shattered. "Ben, why didn't you tell me?"

"I just told you, didn't I?" Ben said, his tone as calm as if he were discussing the weather.

From the piano, a clumsy *plink-plink-plonk* started up again as Zoe resumed her exploration.

Adam's agitation surfaced, his voice straining in disbelief. "At a time like this, you decide to be funny?"

Ben glanced at the piano. He could see Abbey, her back to them, straining to overhear. He turned back to his older brother, who looked genuinely terrified on his behalf.

"I'm not worried, Adam," Ben said quietly. "Sarah and I have enough saved for me to take a break. I was due one anyway." He let that sink in, then added, "I'm thinking about taking the rest of the year off. Spend some more time with Zoe." He nodded toward his granddaughter, who had just managed a recognizable *Twinkle*.

Adam was speechless. He leaned back into the couch cushions, the movement slow and defeated. He ran a hand through his hair, staring at nothing.

You have one final sprint to go, brother, Ben thought, *but I've finished my marathon already.* It wasn't pity he felt, nor pride. It was the quiet acknowledgment of a path long-since chosen.

Finally, Adam let out a hollow laugh. "Wow. Okay." He shook his head, looking at Ben with a kind of baffled awe. "You're just a wrinkly old dragon, aren't you? Sitting on your mountain of gold."

He let out a short, sharp breath, his defensiveness kicking in. "And before you ask, yes, Ben, I do have my own emergency fund."

Ben just smiled.

When the Storm Hits

That cold spike of panic you saw in Adam—his terror on Ben's behalf—is the default state of the script. It's a life of pathetic, brittle fragility, one paycheck away from disaster.

The Builder knows the truth. When you start thinking in generations, setbacks are not a matter of if, but when. A job loss, a market crash, a recession, a health crisis... a storm *will* hit.

The scripted person crosses their fingers and hopes. The Builder prepares.

True wealth isn't the size of your investment portfolio; it's your family's ability to remain secure and unshaken when the storm hits. It's the calm Ben felt when he delivered his news to Adam. This chapter is your guide to forging that resilience. This is how you build the Fortress.

1. The Foundation: Your Emergency Fund

This is the "Fortress Wall" we introduced in the Builder's Waterfall. This is what Ben's calm looked like in practice. It's the non-negotiable, liquid cash buffer that protects your family and your mission from a sudden shock.

How big should your wall be? The answer depends on your risk.

- If your family has dual incomes, you have a built-in redundancy. If one person loses their job, the other income is still covering the "Essentials." Your target is a minimum of 3 months of essential living expenses.

- If your family is single-income, you are the single point of failure. Your target is a minimum of 6 months of essential living expenses.

This is the fund that turns a "crisis" into an "inconvenience." It buys you time to find the right next job, not just the first job. It allows you to handle a $2,000 car repair without blinking or touching your real investments.

2. The Strategic Shield: General Insurance

The scripted person buys insurance out of fear. They have no emergency fund, so a $500 broken car window is a catastrophe. They pay huge premiums for low-deductible policies loaded with bells and whistles, all to cover risks they should be able to cover themselves.

The Builder is different. The Builder uses their emergency fund strategically.

You "self-insure" the small stuff. You intentionally take a higher deductible ($1,000, $2,000) on your home and auto insurance, which dramatically lowers your monthly premiums. That freed-up cash flow goes straight to your "Mortgage Laser." Your robust emergency fund easily covers the deductible if a storm hits.

You reserve your insurance policy for its true purpose: catastrophic, mission-ending events—the house fire, the major liability suit, the things your emergency fund can't handle. They use insurance as a crutch; you use it as a shield.

3. The Time Shield: Health Insurance

The same logic applies to your health. The specifics vary by country, but the philosophy is universal.

The scripted person says, "I can't afford the monthly premium for health insurance."

The Builder asks a different question: "Can I afford to be on a 6-month public waiting list for a hernia surgery, unable to work, while my family's mission grinds to a halt?"

You are the engine of this plan. Health insurance isn't a "cost"; it's a strategic tool you buy to protect your time and your ability to work.

4. The Mission Shield: Income & Disability Insurance

What if the storm isn't temporary? What if a long-term illness or injury takes you out of the game? This is where you must assess your risk in two stages.

The Survival Test: This is the priority. If you are disabled and cannot work, will your family survive? Will they lose the house? If your partner's income or your social safety net is not enough to cover the "Essentials," then income protection is a non-negotiable. You must protect your family from ruin.

The Mission Test: This is the Builder's question. Even if your family can survive, will the mission survive? Your social safety net might keep you alive, but it will not fund your "30% Builder's Waterfall". The "Mortgage Laser" will stop. The "Century Tree" will wither. The entire plan could be delayed by a generation.

The "Scripted" person only asks, "Will I survive?"

The Builder asks, "Will the mission survive?"

It's up to you to decide wisely if you need private insurance to protect the blueprint itself.

5. The Dynamic Backstop: Life Insurance

This logic extends to the ultimate storm: your death. Life insurance is a dynamic shield that protects your family's most vulnerable points.

In the early years of the blueprint, your family is most exposed. Your mortgage is large, your Fortress is small, and your kids are young. Here, your policy is the mission's ultimate backstop. It should be strategically sized to, at a minimum:

- Clear the entire mortgage.
- Fund your children's "Strategic Education".
- Provide a buffer of living expenses for your partner to grieve and find their footing.

But as you follow the blueprint, your Fortress grows. The mortgage shrinks. The kids are educated. The need for that massive policy shrinks with it. Your own wealth is now doing the job the insurance used to do. It is a scaffold you remove as the building becomes strong enough to stand on its own.

6. The Final Command: Your Will

There is one final, unforced error that can destroy all this work: dying without a will. This is the ultimate scripted move—assuming it will all just work out.

It won't. If you die intestate (without a will), you are inviting two new storms into your family's life:

The Legal Storm: The government and the courts, not your partner, will decide what happens to your assets. This can freeze your Fortress for months or years, all while your grieving family is trapped in a legal nightmare.

The Family Storm: It is a legal, open invitation for any distant relative to come out of the woodwork and make a claim on your legacy, draining your Fortress in legal fees.

A simple, legal will is your final act of command. It protects your partner, silences any challengers, and ensures your mission continues unbroken. Don't wait.

Chapter 12
The First Alliance

Scene 9: The First Brick

(Directly after Scene 1)

The red taillights of Adam's car disappeared over the crest of the hill.

Ben stood alone on the pavement, his hands in his pockets. The sound of his brother's engine faded, replaced by the distant, lonely hum of the crossroads. He looked up the dark hill toward Adam's new house, a geometric shadow against the dying light. He felt the weight of his father's words, the pride in a "rite of passage" that he had just recognized as a trap.

A life sentence.

He took a slow breath of the cool night air, the chill sharp in his lungs. Then he turned his back to the street and walked toward the warm, yellow light spilling from his own front window. He crossed the threshold, closing the door and sealing out the night. A new thought, small and sharp, cut through the restlessness.

Then again, maybe we can get out early with good behavior.

The house was quiet save for the sound of shuffling from the kitchen. He found his wife, Sarah, standing amid a happy mess of unpacked boxes. Plates, bowls, and mugs were stacked in precarious towers on the limited benchtop.

She looked up as he entered, a weary, proud smile on her face.

"Well, Mr. Homeowner," she said, her voice cheeky, "I love this place already. But your first official project is to build me some shelves. I've officially run out of room."

Ben smiled, the tension from outside breaking. He walked over, put his arms around her waist, and kissed her. "My first task is to put the kettle on," he said, reaching past her to flick the switch. "But while it boils... what were you thinking? Right here?"

He gestured to an empty wall, and for a few minutes, they planned. They visualized the shelves, their hands sketching in the air as a comfortable, aligned team.

The kettle clicked off. They made their tea and navigated the fortress of cardboard in the living room, settling onto their old couch. The mood was peaceful. It was the quiet of a shared mission just begun.

In the lull, Sarah leaned her head on his shoulder. "What are you thinking about?" she asked, her voice soft. "You've been a million miles away since your dad and Adam left."

Ben took a sip of his tea. "I was just thinking about Adam," he said. "He kept trying to look proud of that new house, but he looked... terrified. He told me it felt like standing at the bottom of a mountain."

Sarah was quiet for a moment. Ben knew she was waiting for him to continue.

"And Dad just gave him a pat on the back. 'Atta boy.' Like it was a great achievement." Ben shook his head, the restlessness returning. "I don't want that for our child, Sarah. I don't want her starting at the bottom of the same mountain."

Sarah shifted, turning to look at him. "Ben, *please*," she said gently, with a small laugh. "We started Sophie's piggy bank before we even knew we were having a girl. She will *not* be starting from the bottom. That's why we bought this place, isn't it? So we'd have a buffer?"

He laughed, a short, relieved sound. "I know, you're right." He leaned back, his mind still working. "It just... it feels like there must be more. Some other way. Something we're missing."

"Like what?" she asked.

Ben finally put words to the new, heavy problem he'd just discovered. "I can't see how it's possible to build Sophie's future while we have our own mortgage mountain to worry about."

Sarah looked at him, her expression practical and clear, the quiet strength he'd always loved. "What's stopping us from doing both?" she said simply. "We can save money for Sophie's future while climbing our own mountain, can't we?"

Ben stared at her. It was so simple. So obvious. Not "either/or". *Both*.

Before he could even respond, Sarah continued. "A plan doesn't start tomorrow, Ben. It starts now. Let's make our first extra mortgage payment. Right now. Even just fifty dollars. Just to draw a line in the sand."

A slow smile spread across Ben's face. He was sparked by her, his partner, his alliance. He pulled out his phone, opened their banking app, and handed it to her.

"You do it," he said.

Sarah took the phone. She found the mortgage account, her fingers tapping with deliberate purpose. She typed in the amount: $50.

She paused, her thumb hovering over the "confirm" button, and looked at him.

He nodded.

She pressed the button.

They sat there for a long time in the quiet, box-filled room, two people in a small house at the bottom of the hill, having just made their first, unified strike against the script.

The First Alliance

The fifty-dollar payment Ben and Sarah made wasn't a number. It was an oath. It was the sound of two people grabbing the same oar and rowing in the same direction. It was the forging of their First Alliance.

And let's be honest: You can't do this alone.

The Old Money Blueprint is a multi-decade mission. It's a siege. It's too hard to do by yourself, and it will be impossible if your most important teammate is still living in the Matrix.

What happens when you come home, "red-pilled" and ready to fight, only to find your partner has just signed a loan for a brand-new SUV? What happens when they are the one who suggests buying a $5,000 "investment" piano for your seven-year-old?

They aren't an antagonist. They aren't a saboteur. They are a prisoner. They are still following the script that society has fed them. The one you just escaped.

Your first mission as a Builder is not to attack your mortgage. It is to stage a rescue.

This conversation is your first, most important test of courage. You can't ambush them. You can't charge in, wild-eyed, and demand they unlearn a lifetime of programming in one night. You've had this whole book to process; they've had zero.

This isn't an ambush; it's a proposal. You must be a strategist.

The "How" and "Why" of the Conversation

Your partner, like all of us, is motivated by two forces: the practical "How" and the philosophical "Why." They are the Yin and Yang of a life-changing decision. You need both, but you must lead with the one that speaks their language.

Your job is to know your partner. Are they a practical, "How-focused" person, or a philosophical, "Why-focused" person?

Path 1: For the Practical, "How-Focused" Partner

This is the partner who loves a spreadsheet, who feels the daily pinch of the budget, who is skeptical of big ideas. Don't lead with the philosophy. Lead with the math.

You Say: "Honey (or pumpkin, cutie-pie, sushi roll, etc), I've been running the numbers. I've found a way we can build a 6-month emergency fund, pay off our mortgage in 7-10 years instead of 30, and still have a dedicated, non-negotiable budget for family holidays."

They Will Say: "That sounds great, but it also sounds like hell. Why would we go that hard? Why not just do what we're doing?"

You Answer with the "Why": "Because this is how we build our Fortress. So our family is finally secure. And it's how we plant the Century Tree, so we can give our kids a real head-start and ensure we're never a burden on them."

Path 2: For the Philosophical, "Why-Focused" Partner

This is the partner who is a dreamer. They get bored by budgets but inspired by a big, emotional mission. Don't lead with the numbers. Lead with the vision.

You Say: "Sushi roll, I just had this profound realization. What if the most important thing we could ever do—our family's real mission—is to give our kids and grandkids a home? The actual, tangible keys to their first home, free and clear?"

They Will Say: "I love that... but how? How on earth could we ever afford to do that? We're drowning in our own mortgage."

You Answer with the "How": "We do it by getting the bank off our back. We do it by following the Builder's waterfall. It's a specific, methodical plan to capture our Lost Harvest and use all that wasted interest for our family, not the bank's shareholders."

The "Generational Fast-Forward"

Once your First Alliance is forged, you can consider the ultimate accelerator.

But first, I have to *sell* you on it.

You've just committed to being the Pioneer. Your ego is tied to that. The idea of asking your parents for help might feel like cheating or failing before you've even started.

But let's be clear. That's the script talking. It's the idiotic "pull yourself up by your bootstraps" narrative that keeps families financially isolated and weak.

This isn't a handout. It's not cheating. It's the single smartest strategic move you can make.

If you can activate your parents, you don't skip the mission. You *fast-forward* it by a generation. You aren't failing as a Pioneer; you are giving your Pioneer parents the opportunity to complete their mission by making you the Bridge.

So how do you have this conversation without sounding like an entitled child?

You don't "ask for money." You "present a strategic proposal."

It starts with the truth. You explain the "Lost Harvest". You explain the "life sentence". You show them the math of what the bank is stealing from their grandchildren.

And then, you make your proposal.

The Proposal: "You are in a position to be the Pioneer for this entire family. If you can help me bypass this 'life sentence'..."

The Contract: "...I will, in turn, become the Bridge. I will commit to this blueprint. Every dollar that would have gone to the bank will be captured and invested in the Century Tree for your grandchildren. This isn't a gift that stops with me. It's a legacy that I will pay forward."

This isn't an 'all-or-nothing' demand. It's a tiered, strategic "ask":

The Best Case (The Liberation Event): "You have the power to liberate us from the life sentence entirely. Can you help us bypass the mortgage trap so we can begin building the Century Tree for your grandchildren today?"

The Good Case (The Rent Hack): "If not, could we live in your investment property for below-market rent? That would allow us to build our Fortress and accelerate the mission, capturing that wealth for the family instead of giving it to a landlord."

The Humble Case (The Launch Pad): "We are serious about this mission, but we've run the numbers and our starting position is tough. We need a launch pad. Would you let our family move into your spare room for one year? It would let us save a deposit, get our Fortress started, and actually launch this blueprint for your grandchildren."

The First Alliance you forge with your spouse is the foundation. This Second Alliance you attempt to forge with your parents is the accelerator.

Both require courage. Both require strategy. This is the work of a Builder.

SKEPTICS CORNER

Q: "This all sounds great, but what if my partner is completely against it? I tried the 'How' and the 'Why,' and they just... said 'no.' Is the whole plan dead?"

No. A "no" is almost never a 100% rejection.

Your partner didn't say "no" to everything. They just said "no" to the parts that sound scary. Come on, they aren't against the idea of saving more money or being more secure, are they?

That's your opening.

Forget the Century Tree. Forget the Liberation Event. Forget the Pioneer. Those are advanced concepts. Your partner is still stuck in the script, and that's okay.

You find the point of agreement. You say, "You're right. Let's forget all the 'generational' stuff. But I think we can both agree we should be saving more for our own retirement, right?"

When they agree, you become the strategist. This is your financial compromise: You say, "Okay. If we're going to save, let's just be smart about it. The most logical, powerful place to put that money is in our tax-advantaged accounts, like our 401(k)s and IRAs. It makes the most sense."

You are both agreeing to build your own Fortress.

But your parenting mission is not a compromise. This is where you must still be the Architect. While you can't force your partner's beliefs, you still have the sacred, non-negotiable duty to shape the world inside your children. You are the one who sets the "family standard". You are the one who models, by your own actions, a life of production over consumption, and teaches them what this blueprint stands for.

Fast-forward 20 or 30 years. You've honored the compromise. You've become your Boomer parents, sitting on a mountain of gold. You are secure.

Now, you get to have a new conversation.

You turn to your partner and say, "We did it. We're secure. Now... what is the most meaningful thing we can do with this? Should we just let it sit here, or could we use it to change our kids' lives?"

You haven't forced them, you've led them. You've given them two decades to see the proof. They are far more likely to agree to the "Liberation Event" when it's a question of "meaning" from a position of absolute security, not a "sacrifice" from a position of scarcity.

Q: "I tried the 'Generational Fast-Forward' conversation. My parents have the money, but they're deeply bought into the script. They said 'no' and told me to 'pull myself up by my bootstraps.' Now what?"

You say, "You're right. Thanks for your time." And then you walk away.

Let's be honest: that conversation was always a long shot. It was a "bonus," not the plan.

This isn't the hill to die on. Don't burn the relationship. Your parents are trapped in the script that worked for them. You won't "red pill" them in one conversation, and you'll only create bitterness by trying.

Your children need a relationship with their grandparents. That relationship is a form of Legacy Capital that is more valuable than a short-term fight about money.

Accept the "no." It's not a failure. It's a clarification.

It clarifies that you are the Pioneer. You are the one who will do this alone. It's what you were planning to do anyway.

So, you thank them for their time. You go home. You look at your partner. And you get to work.

Chapter 13
The Heretic's Guide to Social Pressure

Bonus Scene: The Family Dinner

Mark's fork froze halfway to his mouth.

The dining room was pristine, a museum of 1970s high-status that, in this market, was now a top 1% home. The food was fantastic, the wine was flowing, and the table was heavy with the weight of family history.

"Mark, dear," his aunt said, her voice bright. Her pearls and diamonds caught the light of the chandelier. "I just have to ask, because I love you... Don't you think it's time you bought a real car?"

She let out a small, sharp laugh, dabbing her lips with a cloth napkin. "I was so embarrassed when you pulled into the drive. The neighbors will get the wrong ideas if they see something like that parked here."

The table went quiet. Mark felt a hot, prickling flush creep up the back of his neck. He could feel his mother's eyes on him, sharp and judgmental.

"Oh, leave him be," his dad piped up from the end of the table, waving his own fork. "That old beater is fun to work on, and it's still running like new, despite the... well, despite the rust."

It was a flimsy defense, and it collapsed in an instant.

"Fun isn't the issue, Frank," his uncle chimed in, leaning forward. He was a man who loved to 'just play devil's advocate.' "I'm worried about the safety features, Mark. What's the safety rating on that old thing? You can't put a price on safety."

Before Mark could even respond to his uncle, his mother cut in. Her voice was cold.

"Mark has decided he's too good to buy a car from this century," she said to the table, not to him. "He wants to buy his future kid a house."

The hot flush on Mark's neck turned into a cold sweat. *Mom, not again, not now, please.* He felt cornered, the accusation in her tone making him defensive.

"I never asked you to buy me a house and I never expected you to buy me one," he said, his voice tight. "We've talked about this." He turned to his uncle, trying to regain control with logic. "And it makes no sense to take out a $50,000 loan at 10% interest for an asset that will lose 75% of its value..."

"But you love to rub it in every chance you get, don't you?" his mother snapped, cutting him off. Her eyes were bright. "You refuse to buy a new car. You refuse to look at a nicer house. Just like you refuse to play golf with your dad on the weekend..."

She glanced at her husband, who seemed to sink so deep into his chair he could barely be seen, just the shiny, sweaty top of his bald head.

"You relish in it, don't you, Mark?" she said, her voice rising. "You love rubbing that disgraceful car in our face, like some kind of indictment on our parenting!"

That was it. The killing blow.

Mark looked from his mother's furious, accusatory face to his father, who had all but vanished. He was completely, totally alone. Judged. Confused.

Why don't they understand? he thought, the words a silent plea. *It's just... logic. I'm trying to do something noble...*

But the "why" was a black hole. He had no answer. He broke eye contact, staring down at his plate of now-cold food. The silence was absolute, and then, slowly, his aunt cleared her throat, and the sound of cutlery on porcelain started up again, sealing his defeat.

The Heretic's Guide to Social Pressure

That was the script's immune system in action.

What just happened to Mark wasn't a "family discussion." It was a conformity attack. It was a chaotic, multi-front ambush of status-anxiety (the Aunt), flawed "concern" logic (the Uncle), and deep, personal guilt (the Mother).

Mark was defenseless because he tried to fight an emotional ambush with logic. He failed because he thought the topic was cars, when the real topic was non-conformity. A heretic fights with structure. He didn't have the tools.

You will.

Here is the Heretic's Toolkit for neutralizing social pressure.

The core idea is this: **You cannot fight social pressure with logic**. You must fight it with identity and structure.

Mark's family wasn't looking for a financial calculation; they were demanding emotional conformity. Their "proof" that Mark is wrong is simply that "everyone else is doing it". Their logic is circular. You can't win that argument, so you must make it irrelevant.

Social pressure is the script's immune system. It's not personal; it's a scripted antibody attacking anything it doesn't recognize. Your job isn't to fight the whole system. It's to make yourself invisible to it, deflect it, or build a shield strong enough to withstand it.

Here are the six techniques.

Phase 1: The Internal Shield (Your Mindset)

These are the techniques you practice before the encounter. They are your first line of defense.

Technique 1: "The 'Script-cast'" (Depersonalization)

The Problem: We take social pressure personally. "My mother is attacking me."

The Heretic's Reframe: It's not your mother attacking you; it's the script speaking through her.

The Technique: You learn to see social pressure as a "weather report" for the scripted world. It's predictable, impersonal, and you don't argue with it.

- "When are you buying a house?" → *Ah, the 'script-cast' is calling for 'Financial Conformity' today. Predictable.*
- "That's a 'risky' move." → *I see the 'Career Security' storm front is moving in. Interesting.*

Why it Works: It removes the emotional sting. It's not an attack, it's just noise. You can't be angered by something you've already predicted and depersonalized.

Technique 2: "The 'Mission Shield'" (Your "Why")

The Problem: Their "why" (conformity, safety) is stronger than your "why" (which you haven't defined).

The Heretic's Reframe: Your Mission is your armor.

The Technique: You must have a "Why" that is more compelling than their "Why not?" Before you walk into the family dinner, you review your mission.

- Scripted Aunt: "Why would you quit your stable job to do that?"
- Heretic's Internal Monologue: *She's asking 'why' from a place of fear. My 'why' is freedom, autonomy, and building a legacy for my children. My 'why' is stronger.*

Why it Works: It turns a defense into an affirmation. Their questions become a reminder of why your path is the right one for you.

Phase 2: The External Deflection (Your Actions)

These are the verbal judo moves you use in the moment. You don't meet force with force. You redirect, deflect, and let their energy exhaust itself.

Technique 3: "The 'Grey Rock' Reframe" (Strategic Boredom)

The Problem: You try to explain yourself (like Mark did). This is a fatal mistake. It signals that you accept their authority to judge you.

The Heretic's Reframe: Be polite, be calm, and be unbelievably boring.

The Technique: You give non-answers that are socially acceptable but offer zero emotional or intellectual hooks for them to grab onto.

- Them: "You're still driving that old car? You're just asking for trouble!"
- You: "That's an interesting perspective. I'll have to think about that. Did you try this roast? It's amazing."
- Them: "I just don't think you're saving enough in your 401k."
- You: "I really appreciate you looking out for me. I'm comfortable with my plan." (End of sentence. No further explanation).

Why it Works: You are not a target. You are a "grey rock." An argument needs two people. By refusing to engage, you give their pressure nothing to stick to. They will get bored and find someone else to "fix".

Technique 4: "The Topic Fence" (The Hard Boundary)

The Problem: Some people don't get the hint. They push past your "Grey Rock".

The Heretic's Reframe: You must be willing to build a fence around certain topics.

The Technique: This is a direct, calm, and non-negotiable statement. It is not an attack; it is a rule.

- "Mom, I love you. My finances aren't up for discussion. I'm happy to talk about anything else. How's your garden coming along?"

- "I'm not going to discuss my career choices with you. That topic is off-limits."

Why it Works: It changes the scripted person's calculation. They now understand that if they continue to push, the conversation itself (and their connection to you) is at risk. Most will back down.

Phase 3: The Antidote (Your New World)

This is the long-term, proactive strategy. You can't live in a defensive crouch forever.

Technique 5: "Curate Your Inputs" (The 'Media Fortress')

The Problem: Social pressure isn't just people; it's your Instagram feed, the news, and the shows you watch. You are marinating in the script 24/7.

The Heretic's Reframe: Your mind is your fortress. You are the only one who can guard the gate.

The Technique: A ruthless audit of your "inputs".

- Social Media: Mute, unfollow, or block anyone (even friends) whose content makes you feel scripted pressure.

- News/Media: Stop consuming outrage media that reinforces the script (e.g., "The housing market is a nightmare!" "You'll never retire!").

- Consumption: Actively replace scripted inputs with unscripted ones (podcasts, books, communities) that support your mission.

Why it Works: It starves the script of its main source of power: your attention. You create an echo chamber of your own design.

Technique 6: "Build the Heretic's Council" (The New Tribe)

The Problem: The heretic is alone, and the scripted are many.

The Heretic's Reframe: The only antidote to scripted social pressure is unscripted social pressure.

The Technique: You must find your people. Find the other heretics. They are in masterminds, online forums, and niche communities. This "Council" becomes your new social gravity. They are the ones you go to for advice. Their "why" reinforces your "why".

Why it Works: This is the final move. You haven't just resisted the old gravity; you have left its orbit and entered a new one that pulls you toward your Mission. You are no longer a heretic; you are a pioneer in a new world.

Epilogue

Adam's Legacy

The bank office was old but well-maintained, a time capsule from an era that believed dark wood and brass fixtures conveyed a sense of unbreakable stability. Adam's granddaughter sat alone in a comfortable leather chair, a cup of nice, hot coffee in her hand.

She looked around, taking in the environment. It felt less like an office and more like a holding pen. The kind where animals waited before being milked, or perhaps a holding cell, where criminals waited to see the judge. She couldn't help but notice that the expensive-looking pens on the banker's desk were chained down.

A sudden, bright flash of excitement cut through the unease. She was being too cynical. This was a *good* thing.

Look at me, she thought, a smile touching her lips. *Here. In a bank. Getting my first home.*

It was a symbol of her ambition, a tangible sign that she was capable, that she was making her parents proud. She was *growing up*.

The banker, a friendly man in a nice suit, re-entered the room, holding a thick, freshly printed document. He smiled warmly.

"Sorry about the wait," he said, his voice easy. "The stupid thing sent it to the wrong printer. But, it's all locked in." He placed the contract on the desk in front of her, her official copy.

She looked at the document, then back at him. "Is there... is there anything else to do?"

He chuckled. "Nope. That's it. You are free to go."

The words hit her. *Free to go.* She had just signed her name to a thirty-year obligation, and this man was telling her she was "free." The irony was so heavy it felt like a physical weight, and she didn't stand up right away. She just stared at the contract, lost in a sudden, cold fog.

"Miss?" the banker asked, his smile faltering into concern. "Are you alright?"

She snapped out of it, forcing that bright, capable smile back onto her face. "Oh, yes. Fine," she said, reaching for the papers. She laughed, a quick, sharp sound, and said the strangest thing without knowing why. "It's just... for a second, it felt like a life sentence."

Ben's Legacy

Ben stood in the afternoon sun, his hands resting on the porch rail of a small, new house. He would be eighty his next birthday. His body was not what it had been, the decades of work etched into his joints, but his posture was still straight. His eyes, watching the scene on the lawn, were clear. The fire was still burning.

This house had the same potential he'd seen in his own, all those years ago. He could already see where the fruit trees would go.

His daughter, Sophie, stood beside him. She was a woman in her prime, a calm, strong matriarch, her shoulders back, her presence solid. She was watching her own daughter—Ben's granddaughter, Zoe—who looked on, her face bright with anticipation.

"Okay, okay," Sophie said, and Ben could hear the tears thickening her voice. She stepped forward and put her hands on her daughter's shoulders.

"Zoe, my first daughter," she said, her voice breaking with a joy so profound it was almost painful to witness. "The homeowner."

Zoe laughed, a bright, easy sound, and threw her arms around her mother. "Save the speech for the housewarming party, Mom."

They released the hug, but Sophie kept one hand on Zoe's shoulder. With the other, she placed the set of keys firmly into her daughter's hand.

Ben watched, silent.

He felt it. Not just joy, not just pride. He felt... *vindicated.*

This was the resolution. This was the chord he had been trying to find ever since that night at the crossroads, when his father's proud words had felt so wrong.

His mission was fulfilled.

A wave of profound gratitude washed over him. Gratitude for his wife, Sarah, his steadfast partner in the long, quiet siege. Gratitude for his daughter, who had not just inherited his wealth, but his *philosophy*. And a deep, profound hope for the future he was now, finally, seeing.

He watched Zoe put the key in the lock, her own hand steady.

The chain is unbroken, he thought. *The system works.*

Closing Comments

You've finished the book. Most men won't.

You've seen the script for what it is, and you now know where the exits are.

But insight alone doesn't change outcomes.

Action does.

The next move is yours.

Some men will close this book and return to familiar habits.

Others will make a small, deliberate change — and allow it to compound.

If this book was useful, pass it to a man who needs it.

Ideas like these only work when they move.

See you in the arena.

— Sam Turney

Sam Turney

www.ingramcontent.com/pod-product-compliance
Lightning Source LLC
Chambersburg PA
CBHW032032050726
47590CB00006B/2386

* 9 7 8 1 7 6 4 5 1 1 3 1 5 *